FIFTY EARLY AMERICAN TOWNS

BY EVERETT B. WILSON

South Brunswick
New York: A.S. Barnes and Co., Inc.
London: Thomas Yoseloff Ltd

A.S. Barnes and Company, Inc.
South Brunswick, New Jersey

Thomas Yoseloff Ltd
18 Charing Cross Road
London W.C. 2, England

To Kay and Helen

6376
Printed in the United States of America

ACKNOWLEDGEMENTS

The author is indebted to the following individuals and entities who furnished photographs for use in the book:
Colonial Williamsburg, Virginia
Mrs. Alfred G. Engstrom, Hillsborough, North Carolina
Marblehead Historical Society, Marblehead, Massachusetts
Old Salem, Inc., Winston-Salem, North Carolina
State of Delaware
State of New Jersey
State of North Carolina
Mr. Robert Warner, Washington, Connecticut

The author also is grateful to the curators and owners of houses in which interior photographs were made.

Special credit also is due to the following who assisted in the preparation of the book:
Walter Hard, Sr., Manchester, Vermont
Edward L. Crook, Waterford, Virginia
Mrs. Dora Lee Huston, Waterford, Virginia
John Lewis, Hamilton, Virginia
Mrs. Elgar H. Stabler, Spencerville, Maryland
Miss Marjorie F. Virden, Lewes, Delaware
Miss Caroline Wilson, Oxford, Maryland

Valuable assistance was received from the following: National Park Service, Society for the Preservation of New England Antiquities, Dover Day, One Day in New Castle, Antiquarian & Landmarks Society of Connecticut, Historic Bath Commission, Landmarks Society of York, Maine, and the Waterford Foundation.

Chambers of Commerce in these cities and states were also most helpful:
Bennington, Vermont
Bordentown, New Jersey
Concord, Massachusetts
Marblehead, Massachusetts
Newburyport, Massachusetts
Plymouth, Massachusetts
Washington, North Carolina
Windsor, Connecticut

Finally, Historical Societies provided valuable information and cooperation in:
Andover, Massachusetts
Bucks County, Pennsylvania
Concord, Massachusetts
Danvers, Massachusetts
Durham, New Hampshire
Hillsborough, North Carolina
Kent County, Maryland
Lewes, Delaware
Lexington, Massachusetts

Litchfield, Connecticut

Maryland

Morris County, New Jersey

Newburyport, Massachusetts

Plymouth, Massachusetts

Salem, New Jersey

Stonington, Connecticut

Talbot County, Maryland

Wethersfield, Connecticut

Windsor, Connecticut

Wiscasset, Maine

INTRODUCTION

The 50 communities described and pictured in this book were all small towns at the time of the American Revolution and most of them still are today, if we concede that a place with fewer than 20,000 people can be classed as a town. The exceptions are Danvers, Lexington, Dedham, and Northampton in Massachusetts, Wethersfield in Connecticut, and Old Salem, now part of Winston-Salem in North Carolina. Even though their populations are moderately higher, they were included because they do not give the impression of being large when one visits the area where their older buildings are located.

Of the 50 towns, 11 still have populations of less than 1000, and well over half have fewer than 5000. The 11 smaller places are: Wiscasset and York Village in Maine; Manchester in Vermont; Washington Crossing in Pennsylvania; Oxford and Sandy Spring in Maryland; Waterford, Jamestown, and Yorktown in Virginia; and Bath Town and Brunswick in North Carolina. Two—Jamestown and Brunswick—are no longer inhabited. All are, or were, bona fide towns, except perhaps Washington Crossing, and even that hamlet now has a post office.

There are, of course, older buildings in most of the towns whose photographs do not appear in the book, either because they could not be effectively photographed owing to shade trees, cloudy weather, or other obstacles, or because they had no distinctive architectural or historic appeal to recommend them.

In attributing outlying houses to present-day towns, the author was influenced by the fact that there were relatively few towns in the early days, so that farm and plantation houses out in the countryside were identified to some extent with the nearest town, regardless of distance. In general, old buildings within five miles or so of an established town are considered by the author to have been a part of the town.

Originally, many of the early settlements covered a considerably broader area than they do now. For instance, Windsor in Connecticut embraced West Windsor, Granby, East Granby, Simsbury, East Windsor, South Windsor, Erlington, and parts of Suffield, Bloomfield, and Vernon, which later became separate towns, while Sandy Spring in Maryland in its early days included areas now known as Ashton, Olney, Colesville, Unity, and Brookeville.

The towns are presented, more or less, from north to south; that is, from Wiscasset in Maine to Brunswick in North Carolina. Each state is, however, completed before another is started. Within the towns, buildings or places are, for the most part, listed from north to south and from east to west.

Other smaller communities which have fine old buildings, such as Portsmouth in New Hampshire, Salem and Quincy in Massachusetts, Bristol in Rhode Island, Guilford in Connecticut, Annapolis in Maryland, Fredericksburg in Virginia, Edenton and New Bern in North Carolina, Beaufort in South Carolina, and St. Augustine in Florida, are missing from the book because they were touched on in a companion volume by the same author entitled *America East,* which also covers historic places in all of the larger eastern cities along the coast.

All of the buildings pictured, except the Antiquarian House in Concord, are believed to have been built or started not later than 1820. Nearly 50 are thought to have been built prior to 1700 and over 200 before the Revolution. Only about 50 of the 370 buildings were erected in 1800 or later.

The town histories, the dates of buildings, and the descriptions of the interiors of many of the buildings were mainly obtained from historical, antiquarian, and landmark societies, chambers of commerce, and the state guides prepared or started by the Works Progress Administration during the depression. The dates when the towns were settled or founded were taken from Webster's Geographical Dictionary and the WPA Guides.

The dates of buildings refer to the year, or the approximate year, when the first parts of the structures are believed to have been started. Many of the old places were built in stages. They started with one or two ground-floor rooms and were then enlarged by adding more rooms on the ground floor, building additional floors, and constructing wings, ells, and lean-tos. In some houses, the original part is now a wing or ell.

Dates of the first construction in many cases have been estimated by competent authorities who have analyzed construction methods in the absence of official records. In some instances, the author relied on dates given by the present owner for lack of other information.

Buildings which are regularly open to the public, whether as museums or otherwise, are identified by the notation (Open). The days and hours are not given since they too often vary, owing to the temporary absence of the curator or for other reasons.

Approximate addresses of most of the buildings are listed in the Appendix. In view of changes which occur in the routing of roads and streets, it may be necessary to check locations with local postmasters, neighborhood storekeepers, long-time residents, and retail deliverymen. It should also be remembered that speedometer mileages vary.

In selecting photographs to be used in the book, the tendency has been to favor the more photogenic buildings, but the author also has attempted to give a reasonably balanced impression of each town as a whole. That is why some smaller and plainer buildings and a few that are in a bad state of repair have been included along with the showplaces. In towns where there are numerous old houses but not many grand ones, if any, the selection of photographs suggests that fact.

Because there were relatively few nonresidential buildings other than churches in the early days, most of the photographs are concerned with old houses. Most commercial and manufacturing activities were carried on in homes during those times. Such separate shops and warehouses as were built apparently were not as well constructed as the better houses and did not survive as long, nor did the thousands of poorly built houses.

The photographs were made by the author except where credit is given to others in the list of acknowledgements.

E. B. W.
Bethesda, Maryland

CONTENTS

FIFTY EARLY AMERICAN TOWNS

OUR EARLY TOWNS

Anyone who is curious about how and where his American ancestors lived in colonial times need not rely on history books or reproductions of our early settlements. Despite the passage of nearly 200 years since the Revolutionary War, there still remain today at least six charming towns dating from before that war, which are, or at least give the impression of being, virtually unchanged.

Pictured also in this book are a half-dozen other early communities that have sizeable unspoiled sections built in colonial days, and another nine having one or more streets lined with rows of interesting 18th century homes.

The entire towns that seem unchanged, except perhaps for a small, unobtrusive group of shops, are: Wiscasset and York Village in Maine, Old Deerfield in Massachusetts, Litchfield in Connecticut, Yorktown in Virginia, and Bath Town in North Carolina.

By standing with his back to the stores, which were almost non-existent in colonial times, one easily gets the impression in these six towns that he is back in the 1700's. All that meets the eye are mellow old houses, one or two white churches with tall, slender spires, and rows of majestic trees that shade the streets and line the village common or green.

There are no filling stations or parking lots to be seen, no supermarkets, no garden apartments or ramblers with two-car garages. The eye meets no block-long brick schools, no movie houses or drive-ins, no drug stores, no bar-and-grills or cocktail lounges. Only the ubiquitous rows of parked automobiles detract from the illusion of leisurely colonial living.

With the exception of Old Deerfield, which has no commercial development except a small post office and an inn of colonial design, these early towns (the ones which remain early towns) do have a few business places, but they are off to one side and in no way detract from the old-time effect.

Many who have had the chance to compare these places will agree that Litchfield, though grander than most other early towns, and therefore not wholly typical of colonial villages, ranks number one for overall charm and quality. Its appealing white houses, all of them shaded by huge trees and set well back from the street, are situated on North Street and South Street, which depart in opposite directions from the green. If one were to have the chance to start from scratch and plan an ideal colonial village, it would be hard to improve on the Litchfield of today.

Wiscasset ranks close to Litchfield as a superb New England village, but Bath Town probably is much more representative of early villages.

Interestingly, all of these six unspoiled towns still have populations of fewer than one thousand, except Litchfield which runs over by four hundred.

This group does not include, nor does the book, the interesting replicas of old towns such as Shelburne Museum in Vermont, Sturbridge Village, Plymouth Plantation, and the pioneer village at Salem, all in Massachusetts, the Village Crossroads at Cooperstown in New York, and Greenfield Village in Michigan.

The six old towns that have grown larger without too much change are: Woodstock and Old Bennington in Vermont, Concord in Massachusetts, New Castle in Delaware, Chestertown in Maryland, and Old Salem in North Carolina. Williamsburg in Virginia also might be included, for it is the most spectacular of all, but much of its appeal is the result of the rebuilding and restoration of nearly 150 structures.

Woodstock has its fine old houses close together on or near the green; dignified Old Bennington stands off by itself at one end of a modern town; Concord still has its charming colonial area in the midst of a burgeoning suburban growth: and New Castle has half a dozen square blocks with dozens of eighteenth century dwellings and public buildings, while Chestertown has several square blocks of old places on or close to the bank of the Chester River. Old Salem, a town of great appeal, has its open square with over half of its original buildings close by.

In other old-time towns, the early structures are situated along two sides of one or more "colonial" streets. Such is the case in one of the finest of all—Lexington in Massachusetts—which has all the charm and nostalgic attraction of Litchfield, except that a large town has grown up amidst and around its historic Massachusetts Avenue. Andover, Danvers, Old Newbury, and Marblehead, all in Massachusetts, also have their old-time main streets with numerous colonial buildings, as have Stonington, Windsor, Wethersfield, and Farmington in Connecticut. Windsor and Wethersfield boast more than 100 houses built before 1800. Many of them are unpretentious and modest of size but the numbers nevertheless are impressive.

Other towns represented in the book all have their share of early buildings, but they tend to be scattered here and there about town in such a way that one no longer feels the atmosphere of a colonial settlement.

Few of the houses in these small, early towns even came close to being palatial, although many were reasonably large and handsome. Among the grander houses are: the Nickels-Sortwell House in Wiscasset; Woodbridge and Coventry Hall in York Village; the Colonel Jeremiah Lee Mansion in Marblehead; the Mayflower House and Antiquarian House in Plymouth; the Dexter House in Dedham; the Varnum House in East Greenwich; the Ford Mansion in Morristown; Morven in Princeton; the Read House in

New Castle; Widehall in Chestertown; Radcliffe Manor in Easton; Claymont Court in Charles Town; and the Nelson House in Yorktown.

Even more interesting to many than the grand houses are the very early farmhouses built in the 1600's which still stand today, giving an intimate and fascinating picture of the way people lived when the country was young. Among them are: the Perkins House in York Village; the Garrison House in Exeter; the Coffin House in Old Newbury; the Abbot Homestead in Andover; the Rebecca Nurse House in Danvers; the Hancock-Clarke House in Lexington; the Fairbanks House in Dedham; the Kendall-Holmes, Sparrow, and Harlow Houses in Plymouth; the Frary House in Old Deerfield; the Parsons House in Northampton; the Fyler House in Windsor; the Buttolph-Williams House in Wethersfield; the Whitman House in Farmington; and the Glebe in Woodbury. The colonies to the south had their share also.

Many of the old houses which contain priceless furniture and furnishings are also likely to have splendid hand-carved woodwork in the form of cornices, wainscoting, mantels, stairways, and paneling; a few of the very old farmhouses contain interesting floors, walls, panels, and exposed beams and rafters, all of which have stood the test of age without protective covering. Unusual brickwork is another characteristic of some of the early buildings erected when labor was inexpensive and when prisoners of war, indentured servants, and slaves did the work.

Indeed, some of the humblest old houses, when judged by their exterior appearances, contain surprising examples of wood craftsmanship. Many otherwise modest old houses have at least one mantel with intricate carving and a paneled end-wall in the parlor.

Although many of the old places were lived in by the great and near great in our country's past, there can be no doubt about who added the most luster to houses and taverns around the country. The names one encounters over and over when reviewing the histories of the old houses are those of George Washington and the Marquis de Lafayette. Everywhere they went and stopped they are still remembered today. "George Washington slept here" and "George Washington ate here" are no jests to the present-day owners of the old homes and taverns where he tarried.

A few, but only a few, of the old structures show evidences of neglect, and those for the most part are houses which have little architectural or historic appeal or places still owned by descendants who have come upon lean days financially. Losses from fire can not always be prevented, but ruthless destruction of colonial buildings to make way for new highways, shopping centers, apartment hotels, and subdivisions has been slowed down greatly, and in some places stopped almost completely, by pressure from history-minded organizations.

Historical and antiquarian societies; specialized organizations such as the Society for the Preservation of New England Antiquities, which alone operates more than 40 old buildings as authentically furnished museums; the Daughters of the American Revolution; the Colonial Dames of America; the National Trust for Historic Preservation, and various of the state governments have performed a great public service in protecting, taking over, restoring, and furnishing hundreds of fine old colonial structures.

Proud descendants of colonial owners and other individuals and groups with the necessary resources are also helping to see to it that today's and tomorrow's children will have the chance to see and feel how and where their colonial ancestors and the great leaders of our young nation lived and worked. Thanks to everyone concerned, the roots of the American people are going deeper as each year passes, and their heritage is becoming more secure.

WISCASSET

MAINE

In its early days, Wiscasset was the largest port north of Boston. Located on the west bank of the Sheepscott River, it remained a fairly important port until around 1850 with a good trade in lumber for its sailing ships. At its peak, as many as one hundred "large" ships could dock there at one time.

Its larger homes were built and occupied by affluent shipping merchants and ship captains, but the population began to dwindle when other ports supplanted it, and individuals with an artistic and literary bent began to take over the homes once lived in by shipping folk.

Many of the early houses were built by ship's carpenters, who gave them superior strength and durability, sometimes sacrificing a comparable beauty.

As part of a larger town named Pownalborough until 1795, Wiscasset first was settled in the early 1700's, but that settlement was abandoned during King Philip's War, a prolonged struggle with an Indian tribe. The permanent settlement began in 1730.

The first re-settler was Robert Hoover. William Groves and Robert Lambert came a year later.

Wiscasset retains all the original charm of an early New England town, built up around a sloping green, and shaded by huge trees. Its modest commercial development has not impinged in any way on the old residential area, as it is located down near the water front at one end of Main Street.

Lee-Payson-Smith House. Judge Silas Lee was the first owner of the handsome house with the semi-elliptical porch, supported by Ionic columns. It was built in 1792. Afterward it became the property of General David Payson and was then used as a bank. Governor Samuel E. Smith bought the house in 1836 and it later became a tavern called the "Bunch of Grapes," in which a dancing school was conducted.

Nickels-Sortwell House. The first owner of the house, the grandest in Wiscasset, was Captain William Nickels, a man of wealth and a master mariner. It was erected in 1807 at the then formidable sum of $14,000. Cornelius Turner purchased it in 1820 and operated it as Turner's Tavern. Later it was known as the Mansion House, Belle Haven, and the Wiscasset House. By 1870 it had become dilapidated. It was then renovated and again operated as a tavern before being sold to A. F. Sortwell. The house, known for its Palladian window and lunette window, is now a splendid museum. (Open)

Nickels-Sortwell House. The paneled door with its rounded top opens into a stairhall on the first floor.

Nickels-Sortwell House. The graceful stairway winds up two flights. It is said to have taken two years to construct the staircase and stairhall.

Nickels-Sortwell House. This chest-on-chest, one of many handsome pieces of old furniture seen throughout the house, stands in the drawing room.

Nickels-Sortwell House. Above the window seats in the drawing room are folding and divided shutters.

Thomas W. Smith House. Colonel John Kingsbury built the dark frame house, located away from the green, in 1763. It is the oldest house in town and was once located where the Nickels-Sortwell house is now situated. Dr. Philip Theobold also lived there.

Lilac Cottage. The house, now an antique shop, was built in 1789 by Benjamin Colby. It has white oak beams measuring 14 by 16 inches.

Marsten House. This well-shaded house was built in 1785 for Colonel Alexander Erskine. Colonel Erastus Foote was a later occupant.

Merean House. Francis Cook, collector of customs and a friend of George Washington, built the house in 1795. It had 17 fireplaces.

Village Green. The Congregational Church and the Courthouse overlook the spacious green, side-by-side.

Taylor House. The large frame house was erected in 1780 by Henry Hodge on land that had been owned by William Groves, the early settler, who originally built a log cabin on the site.

YORK VILLAGE

MAINE

Although it originally was founded in 1624 by the Plymouth Company under the name of Agamenticus, York Village in the southeast corner of the state owes its early growth to Scottish prisoners of war who were sent to the colonies as bond servants by Oliver Cromwell. Twelve of the prisoners settled in the village, the first being Alex Maxwell, who had been sold to George Meader of Berwick, Maine. Maxwell went there in 1657 after having discharged his obligations as a bondsman.

The first settlers came under the leadership of Captain William Gorges and Colonel Francis Norton. Thomas Gorges was the first mayor.

Edward Godrey built the first house in 1630. His early neighbors were Walter Norton and Edward Johnson. Other prominent early citizens were: Abraham Preble, soldier, magistrate, and arbitrator; the Reverend George Burdette, called an evil man by one historian, a description which is presumably supported by the fact that one of his feminine followers was required to do penance by standing publicly in the congregation adorned with only a white sheet for two Sabbath Days and in General Court for one day; Henry Sayward, a millwright who became a large owner of land; the Reverend Samuel, a Harvard graduate, said to be well-equipped to "beautify sinful men and raise up the pillars of a prostrate church in troublous times," and the Honorable David Sewall, a judge.

The little village has also been known as Old York and was called Georgeana when it was briefly under the aegis of Sir Fernandino Gorges, an English soldier and mariner who received a grant of land between the Piscataqua and Kennebec Rivers in 1629.

Before the Revolution, York Village had a small "tea party" of its own when a group of citizens known as the Sons of Liberty siezed 150 pounds of tea from the sloop *Cynthia*.

In 1811, the first cotton mill in the state was constructed in the village.

Coventry Hall. Judge David Sewall built the large house in about 1794. President Monroe was among the many distinguished guests who were entertained there. It has fine carved woodwork, and its entrance door has a fanlight framed by slender columns.

Woodbridge. The older part of this charming house was built in about 1740, and the front was added by Edward Emerson, Jr., in 1794. It is known for its captain's walk which extends across the front of the house.

The Pillory. This old-time device for punishing wrong-doers stands in the village green in front of the old jail built in 1653 by the Massachusetts Bay Colony. The jail served as the prison for the whole State of Maine until 1760.

Hugh Holmes House. The frame salt-box, now an antique shop, was constructed in 1727. (Open)

Hugh Holmes House. This beautiful colonial furniture is placed in the parlor.

The Old School. The little school-
house, built in 1745, contains old-time
school furniture.

Steven Lovejoy House. The house,
built in 1751, served for a time as the
Matthew Lindsay Tavern.

John Hancock Wharf. The old wharf and warehouse, erected in 1787, is said to have been the property of John Hancock, patriot and first signer of the Declaration of Independence. (Open)

Elizabeth Perkins House. The original part of this spendid old frame house was probably built in about 1682 by Timothy Yeales. Joseph Holt constructed the front part in about 1730. It is now a beautifully furnished museum, named for a late owner. (Open)

Elizabeth Perkins House. The original built-in corner cupboard contains rare old china.

Elizabeth Perkins House. The kitchen-dining room contains a comparatively small fireplace with crane and oven, a collection of pewter and old silver.

Elizabeth Perkins House. The house is well-equipped with cupboard and shelf space, too often lacking in old homes.

Elizabeth Perkins House. Period antiques, like the graceful table and chair, can be seen in every room.

Elizabeth Perkins House. The narrow front stairway, just inside the entrance, makes two sharp turns above unfinished paneling. On the floor is a leather fire bucket.

DURHAM

NEW HAMPSHIRE

A series of Indian massacres plagued Durham in its early days. First called Oyster River, the name of the stream on which it is situated, the town was settled in 1635 by men from Dover Point.

The initial attack occurred in 1675 during King Philip's War. The most serious raid came in 1694 when more than 100 persons were killed or captured in an attack in which the Indians burned all but five garrison homes. Again in 1704, fifty inhabitants were killed and many were taken prisoner in another Indian war.

Two soldiers—General John Sullivan and Colonel Alexander Scammel—were the town's most prominent citizens in the early years. General Sullivan led a raiding party that seized more than one hundred barrels of powder, plus guns and cannon, from the British at nearby Newcastle in December of 1774. They ferried it down river on fishing boats to Durham, where the cache was hidden in a Meeting House. Ice had to be cut in the frozen Oyster River to permit passage of the craft.

The General, a lawyer, was also a member of the Continental Congress and later served as President of New Hampshire before it became a state.

Colonel Scammel became George Washington's adjutant general during the Revolution, and received a mortal wound at the Battle of Yorktown. Years later, when Lafayette visited America, he proposed a toast to Scammel at a meeting of veterans of the Revolution. Bridges over nearby rivers have been named for the two patriots.

Since 1893, Durham has been the home of the University of New Hampshire.

Demerritt Homestead. The spacious farmhouse situated in a grove of tall trees was built in the late 1700's north of town.

Valentine Smith House. The famous evangelist, the Reverend George Whitfield, is said to have dined in the town house erected in 1735.

Ebeneezer Smith House. Situated next to the Valentine Smith house, this dwelling, known for its blue-domed porch, was built in 1750.

Judge Frost House. The old portion of the house, located on a hill alongside the Oyster River, was built by Valentine Hill in 1649. It was one of the few garrison houses that escaped burning in the Indian raids.

Yatten. The modest frame dwelling, erected in 1789, is perched on the side of the hill between the Judge Frost House and the river.

General Sullivan House. On a slope rising from the Oyster River across from the Frost House, the home of the General of the Revolution was built in 1716 and purchased by him in 1764. Claiming to be a descendant of English-hating Irishmen, the General was a devoted advocate of independence.

EXETER

NEW HAMPSHIRE

Most widely known today as the home of Phillips Exeter Academy, established there in 1781, Exeter was dominated in its early days by the personality of an advocate of unorthodox doctrine, the Reverend John Wheelwright. The Reverend went there from Boston after his college days at Cambridge University in England, where he was a fellow student with Oliver Cromwell.

Wheelwright secured a deed for 400 square miles of land from the Squamscott Indians, but all except 17 square miles later split off as newly established towns separated from Exeter.

Anne Hutchinson, a follower of Wheelwright and his sister-in-law, was exiled from Massachusetts and led a party of 30 fellow heretics to Exeter, where they settled.

The town, which was settled in 1638 by Edward Hilton and others, is located ten miles inland from the Atlantic Ocean on the Squamscott River and, in its early days, was a fishing, lumbering, and shipbuilding center. After the Revolution, it gradually became a small industrial and agricultural community.

Its citizens, who were prominent in the Revolution, also fought in the French and Indian Wars, but there were no important attacks made on the town.

Members of the First Provincial Congress of New Hampshire met there in 1774, and in 1775 the capital was moved from Portsmouth to Exeter. It was in Exeter in 1776 that the First Provincial Congress adopted a written constitution under which New Hampshire became an independent colony. The legislature met there, with few exceptions, from 1776 to 1784.

Prominent among its early citizens was Nicholas Gilman, Jr., one of the 39 signers of the Constitution of the United States.

Governor Weare House. Built in 1748, the handsome house in nearby Hampton Falls was the home of Meschech Weare, a president of New Hampshire and its first Governor. A monument which stands in town bears this inscription: "He was one of those good men who dare love their country and be poor." Both George Washington and Lafayette were entertained here.

Garrison House. Councillor John Gilman built this, one of the very earliest houses in New Hampshire, in about 1650 as a fort to withstand Indian attack. A portcullis was poised over the front door. While a student at Phillips Exeter Academy, Daniel Webster boarded there with the family of Ebeneezer Clifford, a noted wood carver, who carved the paneling for the house that is now displayed in the Metropolitan Museum of Art in New York City. (Open)

Garrison House. A richly furnished dining room is one of the numerous surprises in the early house.

Garrison House. A collection of pewter coffeepots is shown on the shelf of the hand-carved mantel.

Garrison House. Excellent china platters and a gate-leg table appear in a corner of the dining room.

Garrison House. Interior partitions are made of unusually wide rough planks.

Garrison House. Cut-away construction shows the heavy timbers used in the sturdy outer wall construction.

Garrison House. The elaborate bed stands under a massive ceiling beam in an upstairs bedroom.

Garrison House. Another bedroom contains a delicate four-poster in a paneled corner.

Congregational Church. The beautiful white edifice was erected in 1798. (Open)

Benjamin Clark Gilman House. The doorway of the long house, built in the late 18th century, is well off center.

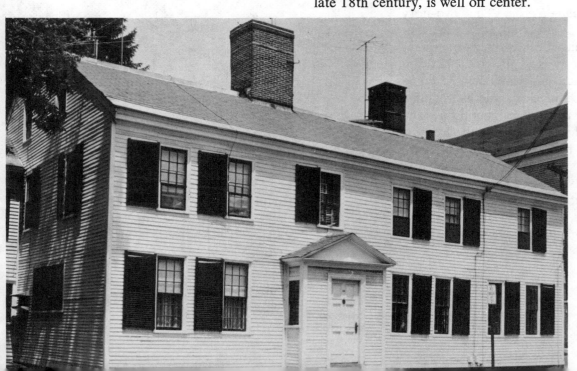

First Academy Building. The little building, erected in 1783, once housed all of the school's activities. It later became the Faculty Club.

Ladd-Gilman House. The two-story house has two vestibules, indicating that it once may have been two separate establishments. It was built in 1721 by Nathaniel Ladd and was later the home of Nicholas Gilman, Jr., who as treasurer of the colony issued New Hampshire currency from the house during the Revolution. It was built of brick, which later was covered with siding laid on large planks, as the stripped portion of the front wall shows. The interior has deep window seats, paneled wainscoting, and huge fireplaces. (Open)

Lyford Farmhouse. A farmer and weaver named Francis Lyford lived in the house, which was built near town in the early 1700's.

WOODSTOCK
VERMONT

This charming New England village of less than 2000 persons lies on the bank of the Ottauquechee River. The land was granted in 1761 and was settled in 1765 by Timothy Knox, a Harvard graduate. Its first clergyman, Aaron Hutchinson, also was a Harvard man and is remembered because his preaching had a powerful effect on Ethan Allen, a fighting man whom other preachers had found hard to impress.

Woodstock is widely admired for its slender village green, around which are located a number of fine old homes. It became a shire town, or county seat, in 1794 and has remained such ever since. At one time the little village boasted five weekly newspapers simultaneously, but the number later dwindled to one.

Woodstock also is known for its prom-inent citizens of earlier days. One was Alvin Adams, once a hostler's assistant at a tavern. He later inaugurated express stage-coach service in 1827 from Woodstock to Windsor, thus starting the Adams Express Company which at one time was an organization of high prestige and international scope.

The town also boasts of John Collander, a member of both the U.S. House of Representatives and the Senate, and also a Postmaster General. George P. Marsh was a member of the House and later served as U.S. Minister to Turkey and Italy. Hiram Powers, a local farm boy, became a famous sculptor. Three of his busts are in the National Capitol in Washington, those of John Marshall, Benjamin Franklin, and Thomas Jefferson.

Dana House. The house with an attractive entrance owned by the Woodstock Historical Association was built in 1807 by Charles Dana. It is furnished with excellent local antiques. (Open)

Dana House. A closet full of old gowns and a washstand are found in a second floor bedroom.

Dana House. Interesting old furnishings are seen in every room.

Swan House. The brick house with the long white fence and elaborate entrance was the home of Benjamin Swan. It was built in 1801.

Kidder House. The square house built in 1807 stands out for the ornamentation on its facade, which is frame, while the end walls are made of brick.

Hutchinson House. Located at the head of the village green, the house erected in 1794 now is part of an inn. It presumably was the home of Aaron Hutchinson, the clergyman. (Open)

Richards House. Captain Israel Richards lived in the frame house with the large central chimney, built on the green in 1787.

William Dimon House. Now a private residence, built in the early 1800's, the house located on the oval village green was once a school.

Parker House. At one time a tavern operated by one Tillie Parker, the low-roofed house built in 1807 now is the headquarters of the local D.A.R. It, too, is on the green.

MANCHESTER

VERMONT

At the time of the Revolution, Manchester, which lies north of Bennington, not far from the New York State border, served as an unofficial capital of the independent State of Vermont, and the state's first Council of Safety met there.

It was in Manchester that Ira Allen, brother of Ethan and an active politician in the Revolution, announced a plan for financing Vermont's Revolutionary activities by confiscating the estates of Tory sympathizers. One of those Tories, Jeremiah French, was a large land owner in the immediate area and was escorted to the Canadian border by the "Green Mountain Boys" when his holdings were taken over by the independent state.

Colonel Seth Warner's regiment camped near Manchester for a few weeks after the Battle of Hubbardstown in the west central part of the state and before the important Battle of Bennington.

Samuel Rose built the first log cabin in Manchester in 1764 and erected the first frame house in 1769. Samuel Purdy was the first male child born there, arriving in 1771.

Otherwise, Manchester's history centers around its attractions as a resort and art center and its distinguished visitors. Mrs. Abraham Lincoln and Mrs. U. S. Grant both visited there, and Robert Todd Lincoln died nearby. Lincoln's granddaughter, Mrs. Charles Isham, was a resident. It also is the home of Walter Hard, the Vermont poet.

Because it is situated near some of Vermont's principal marble quarries, in the shadow of Equinox Mountain, Manchester's sidewalks are paved with large sawed marble slabs.

The Old Tavern. Now an antique shop and guest house, the roadside tavern in Manchester Center was erected about 1790. (Open)

The Grist Mill. The old mill built just off the main street in 1780 is perched above a high dam.

1811 Tavern. Although the present owner believes that the early part of the tavern was built shortly after 1700, the name-sign is more conservative. It formerly was known as the Old Mansion House and is where Lincoln's granddaughter once lived.

1811 Tavern. A fine mantel and over-mantel grace the main parlor.

1811 Tavern. Interesting carving appears above a parlor door.

The Green. Manchester's narrow but graceful green contains a large white marble statue.

Equinox House. Part of this now large hotel was built prior to the Revolution. It faces the green. (Open)

Hoyt House. An unusually long yellow frame building, Hoyt House was started in 1769.

Hard Homestead. This imposing farmhouse, located in the nearby countryside, was built in the 1700's and was the home of the well-known Hard family.

Hard House. The present home of the poet, Walter Hard, is one of the oldest houses in town, having been built in the 1760's.

Governor Galusha House. The house is believed to have been built in the late 1700's by Lavius Fillmore, a church designer who had been a pupil of Charles Bulfinch, the early American architect. It was the home of Jonas Galusha, a Revolutionary officer, and nine times the Governor of Vermont. A nail maker by trade, he made all of the nails and hardware used in the house. It later became a tavern but today it is the home of a descendant of the General.

BENNINGTON

VERMONT

Named for Governor Benning Wentworth of New Hampshire, who charted most of the Vermont territory, Bennington is the oldest town in the state. It lies on the banks of the Walloomsac River in the southwest corner of Vermont, just east of the New York border and north of the Massachusetts line.

It was settled in 1761 by Captain Samuel Robinson of Massachusetts, who had been attracted to the pleasant site while camping there during the French and Indian War.

It was the headquarters of the "Green Mountain Boys," known in New York State as the "Bennington Mob." Their meeting place was the Green Mountain Tavern, later known as Catamount Tavern.

The major event in the town's history occurred in 1777 when British General John Burgoyne began a push down the Champlain Valley, taking Ticonderoga and Mount Independence without a struggle. Needing supplies and horses, he dispatched troops to obtain them in Bennington and other nearby towns. The force of 800 men, including musicians, was composed of British, Tories, Hessians, Canadians, and Indians.

However, colonial forces totalling 1800 militia and volunteers under Colonels John Stark and Seth Warner smashed the invaders, taking 600 prisoners. Two hundred of the enemy were left dead on the field of battle, while the colonials lost only 30 men killed and 40 wounded.

The Bennington engagement was a tremendously important victory, termed by some authorities a turning point of the Revolution. It unquestionably was a crushing defeat for the British and led to their decisive rout at Saratoga shortly afterward.

Pottery, for which Bennington is famous, was made there as early as 1793 when Captain John Norton started a small pottery business which remained in the family for over 100 years.

Governor Galusha House. Walls of the second-floor rooms are decorated with hand-painted designs, as seen over the mantel. The designs were applied shortly after the house was built.

Monroe-Hawkins House. Built in about 1820, the Georgian structure of 24 spacious rooms has marble lintels over its fireplaces and numerous chimney cupboards. Fillmore is said to have designed this house also. Joshua Monroe, the first owner, hanged himself in his barn on account of indebtedness.

Frost House. The stone house, built in 1769, stands on the crest of a hill. For a time it was the home of Robert Frost, the noted poet.

The Battle Monument. The 306-foot spire of Vermont granite, which commemorates the Battle of Bennington, rises from the summit of a broad hill and affords a marvellous view of the rolling countryside. (Open)

Robinson House. The eighth son of Captain Samuel Robinson built the house in 1795. General David Robinson, who later lived there, was a man of great physical strength, and was a private in the Battle of Bennington but he later rose to major-general of the militia.

First Congregational Church. Lavius Fillmore designed this charming church with its wooden quoins and Palladian windows. Built in 1806, it has pewter candle-holders in every pew. (Open)

First Congregational Church. A double stairway leads to the high pulpit under one of the Palladian windows.

Dewey House. This house, believed to be the oldest frame dwelling in the state, was built in 1763 by Jebediah Dewey, an outspoken clergyman and accomplished carpenter, who during a service once called Ethan Allen a blasphemer and ordered him to sit down.

Tichenor Mansion. The first owner of the house, which sits on a knoll back of the inn, was Isaac Tichenor, a Princeton graduate who served for 11 years as Governor of Vermont and was a prominent Federalist statesman. It was erected in about 1790.

Walloomsac Inn. The large gray hostelry was started in 1766 by Captain Elijah Dewey, son of the parson and a veteran of the Battle of Ticonderoga. (Open)

OLD NEWBURY
MASSACHUSETTS

Yankee perseverance and ingenuity are exemplified in Old Newbury, which has seen more than its share of vicissitudes since it was settled by Puritans in 1635. The settlers went there on the order of Governor John Winthrop to prevent the occupation of the region by trappers and other interlopers who were not welcome within the boundaries of the Massachusetts Bay Colony.

The first settlers attempted to farm the area on the water-front now now known as Old Newbury or Newbury Old Town. When that didn't work out they moved up to what is now called Newburyport, the largest present-day community in the original Old Newbury area, which also included the village now known as plain Newbury and also West Newbury.

The location at the mouth of the then navigable Merrimack River was ideal for the early industries—trapping and fishing, whaling, and ocean commerce. Since there was an inexhaustible supply of lumber, ship-building and ocean trade in lumber burgeoned rapidly. In the 60 years after 1681, Old Newbury launched 107 ocean-going vessels and, to support that industry, ironworks, sail lofts, rope-walks, and ships' chandleries sprang up on the busy water-front.

The first setback came when the British imposed heavy duties on ocean commerce before the Revolution. After the war, the British exclusion of American ships from the West Indies trade and from the fishing banks of Newfoundland, and the Jeffersonian shipping embargo, flattened the town's economy.

As if that weren't enough, in 1811 a disastrous fire burned 15 acres in the heart of town, and the new nation imposed heavy tariffs to protect its growing textile industries, which soon wiped out Old Newbury's ocean trade with England, India, and Russia.

Ship-building made a strong comeback in the 1840's with the growing demand for clipper ships, and Old Newbury turned out a number of packets known for their superior performance.

However, the trend toward steamships and the gradual formation of bars and shoals in the harbor, which became clogged with sand, put an end to Old Newbury as a maritime city. It survived only because its imaginative leaders turned to modern manufacturing as a source of income.

The town boasts that it is the birth-place of the U. S. Coast Guard and that the first U.S. commissioned ship, the U.S.R.C. Massachusetts, was launched there in 1791.

Short House. The old frame house with brick ends, started in 1717, has an unusual doorway. It now is an attractive farmhouse museum. (Open)

Short House. An entire end-wall of the parlor is paneled in pine.

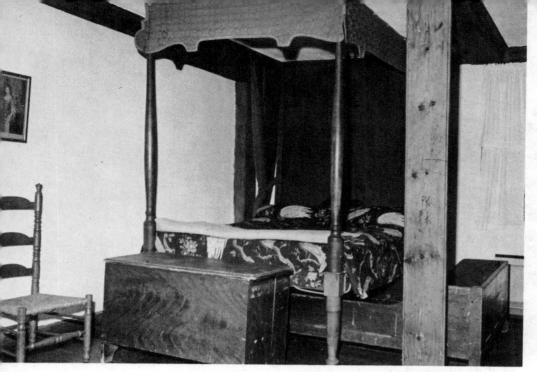

Short House. A sturdy post supports a ceiling beam in the middle of an upstairs bedroom.

Coffin House. The first part of the unpainted farm home was built around 1653. It remained in the Coffin family for almost 300 years. Among those who lived there was Joshua Coffin, historian of Old Newbury. (Open)

Coffin House. Built-in cupboards are an unusual feature over the kitchen fireplace with its swinging crane.

Coffin House. The early kitchen cabinet contains a fine display of pewter plates and platters.

Coffin House. The low interior door with the wooden latch and strap hinges is not much taller than the child.

Cushing House. This was the home of Caleb Cushing, a statesman who entertained John Quincy Adams in 1837. Built in 1808, it is now a museum with interesting woodwork and furnishings, maintained by the Newburyport Historical Society. (Open)

Pettingell-Fowler House. John Pettingell built the large frame house in about 1792. It has a fine mantel.

Moseley House. Recognizable by the ballustrade which runs completely around the roof, the house was erected in 1811.

Jackson-Dexter House. Built in 1771, this was the home of the eccentric "Lord" Timothy Dexter, whose career was traced by John P. Marquand, the noted local author. Dexter is said to have sold New England bed-warming pans to buyers in the tropical West Indies for use as molasses ladles. The chimneys of the house are wood-encased. It now is an office building.

Courthouse. The massive brick structure on the green known as Bartlett Mall is the courthouse erected in 1800. (Open)

The Old Jail. Notable for the row of sharp iron spikes visible along the stone wall in front, the old jail was built in 1744 and used as such until 1825. In the War of 1812, captured British privateersmen were confined there. (Open)

ANDOVER

MASSACHUSETTS

The early history of Andover is largely the story of Samuel Phillips, who operated powder mills there for the Continental Army before and after the Revolution, until they were destroyed by explosions. He later established a paper mill.

But of even greater importance, in 1778 he established there the highly esteemed Phillips Andover Academy, the oldest incorporated school in the United States, just seven years after he was graduated from Harvard. He later became the lieutenant governor of Massachusetts.

Among the many eminent graduates of the Academy are Samuel F.B. Morse, Oliver Wendell Holmes, Josiah Quincy, and George Herbert Palmer.

The town was settled in 1643, when the land was purchased from Indians by John Woodbridge. It then was known as Cochechewick and was renamed for the English home of the early settlers.

Among those early settlers were Simon Bradstreet, son of a non-conformist minister; John Osgood, one of the founders of the church, in whose house the first town meeting was held; and George Abbot, first of the prolific Abbot family, whose wife lived to the then amazing age of 82. All arrived before 1644.

As was done in numerous other places, Andover planted mulberry trees to produce food for silkworms in a futile attempt to produce silk. It gradually developed other industries but education is its number-one preoccupation.

Isaac Abbot Tavern. One of six Abbot houses, it was built in 1680. George Washington had breakfast there in 1789 and is said to have kissed the inn-keeper's daughter, Priscilla, as a reward for mending his gloves. It also was the first Post Office in Andover.

Samuel Abbot House. The large house was built in 1792 with the aid of a design developed for a house in England.

John Lovejoy Abbot House. Once part of the homestead of George Abbot, II, the house was erected in 1678.

Solomon Higgins-Abbot House. This was the homestead of George Abbot, II, who settled in Andover in 1678. The house now standing was built in 1734. The home of the first George Abbot is located across the street.

Bulfinch Hall. The large ivy-covered building on the Phillips Andover campus was built in 1818 and named for Charles Bulfinch, its designer, who was the first professional architect in America.

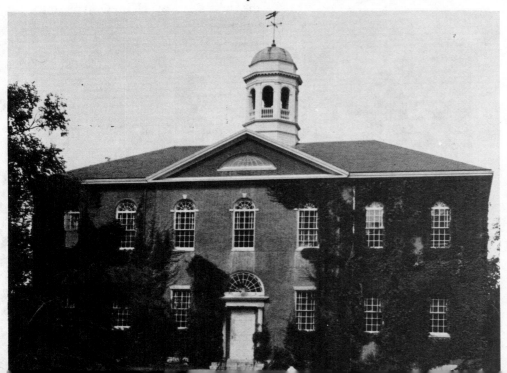

Pearson Hall. Formerly known as Bartlett Chapel, this is another academy building designed by Bulfinch and built in 1818. Its cupola is considered a masterpiece.

Moses Stuart House. William Bartlett built the house in 1812. It later was the home of Professor Moses Stuart, the "Father of Hebrew Literature in America," an eminent scholar who introduced the first font of Hebrew type into the country.

Blanchard House. Deacon Amos Blanchard built the house in 1819 on land purchased from the South Parish. It later was occupied by Deacon Edward Taylor and by Dr. Selah Merrill, U.S. Consul at Jerusalem for many years. It now is a museum of the Andover Historical Society. (Open)

Blanchard House. The handsome sideboard and chairs are seen in the dining room.

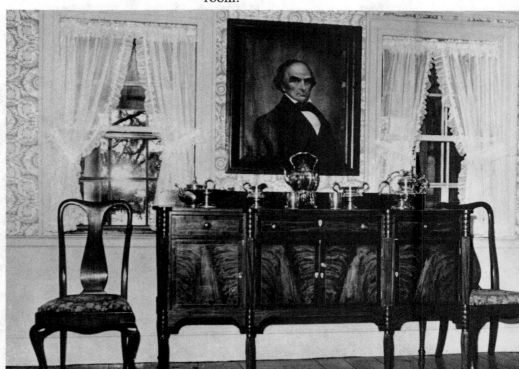

Blanchard House. One of the bedrooms contains this old rocker and carved chest.

Blanchard House. These pieces in the parlor are typical of the splendid "period" furniture in the house.

Poor-Perry House. Deacon Daniel Poor built the house in about 1763. It was later occupied by Captain Oliver Perry, son of the Commodore, a hero of the War of 1812.

Abbot Homestead. The weathered and sagging farmhouse, integrated with the shed and barn, was built in 1685 by Benjamin Abbot, who settled in Andover in 1636. The homestead, which is believed to be the oldest house in town, remained in the possession of his descendants for eight generations. In 1835, when school and church buildings were closed to them, the house was used by students for abolitionist meetings.

MARBLEHEAD
MASSACHUSETTS

Taking its name from the mass of rock on which it is built, Marblehead rests on a peninsula jutting into the Atlantic Ocean, north of Boston and south of Salem.

It was settled in 1629 by fishermen from Cornwall and the Channel Islands. They enjoyed an early prosperity at their calling but it was short-lived because of increasing competition, even though they were aided by Parson John Barnard who helped develop a trade in dried fish with the West Indies and Europe.

Seafaring activity perked up in 1774 when Marblehead became a Port of Entry, after the passage of the oppressive Boston Port Bill which prompted Boston merchants and ship owners to turn to its port as a substitute.

As war approached, the town began to blaze with patriotism. The Old Town House thundered with revolutionary speeches, and Tory merchants who an-ticipated what was ahead started to flee the town as tension heightened. Seafaring men turned to privateering as a source of wealth as war came, but the effectiveness of the British blockade made that form of activity unprofitable. Gradually, Marblehead's economy began to flatten and by the end of the war its ships had been either captured or sunk or else were rotting beside the wharves.

After the war, the fishing fleet was rehabilitated with the aid of lotteries, but then the War of 1812 came with its embargo, and fishing never recovered. Attempts at industrialization were stifled by competition, and the town experienced slow times until it finally developed into a popular yachting center and resort. The harbor then became filled with sleek-hulled yachts, instead of fishing boats, and Marblehead began to talk of itself as the "Yacht Capital of the World."

Pitcher House (The Old Brig). Timbers from a wrecked brigantine were used to build the house in 1720. Later, it was the home of Moll Pitcher, a psychic fortune teller.

Orne House. The large three-story house was the home of Colonel Azor Orne, a wealthy merchant and a member of the Revolutionary Congress of Safety, along with Elbridge Gerry, John Hancock, and Samuel and John Adams. It was erected in 1768.

Barnard House. Built in the early 1700's, the house was named for Parson Barnard, preacher in the First Church, who refused the presidency of Harvard University, and the man who aided the fishing industry. He is said to have returned to Boston every year to spend his birthday in his birthplace.

Devereux House. This was the home of John Devereux, one of Marblehead's early inhabitants. It was built in 1727.

Glover House. Here was the home of General John Glover, built in 1762. He was the first general of Marines, whose men rowed George Washington's army across the Delaware before the Battle of Princeton and across the East River after the Battle of Long Island. His privateer vessel *Hannah* became the first ship of the U.S. Navy.

Old Town House. This town hall predates Faneuil Hall and is known as Marblehead's "Cradle of Liberty." Built in 1727, it was the scene of many turbulent pre-Revolutionary meetings and patriotic gatherings.

St. Michael's Church. This may be the oldest Episcopal edifice in New England, having been built in 1714. Its bell cracked when sounded at the news of the Declaration of Independence, and was re-cast by Paul Revere. (Open)

83

Lafayette House. The corner of the house, built in the early 1800's, was cut away to permit the passage of Lafayette's carriage when he visited Marblehead in 1824. Obviously, the street must have been less commodious to vehicular traffic in those days.

Colonel Jeremiah Lee House. This Georgian mansion is one of New England's finest and most richly furnished and decorated houses. It was erected in 1768 by Colonel Lee, a patriot and wealthy merchant, who imported the materials from many parts of the world. The mansion now is owned by the Marblehead Historical Society. (Open)

Lee Mansion. The drawing room is famous for its excellent paneling and beautifully carved mantel.

Lee Mansion. Splendid murals adorn the walls of the house.

Lee Mansion. The dining room contains fine colonial furniture, together with a wide cornice and wainscoting.

Lee Mansion. The magnificent stairway rises from a broad central hall, lined with wallpaper brought from England with the paneling in Colonel Lee's ships.

Hooper-Parker House. This was the home of Robert Hooper, member of a prominent local family. It was erected prior to 1775.

Colonel William R. Lee House. Here is another pre-Revolutionary house. It was the home of Colonel William R. Lee, a merchant prince, ship owner, and Revolutionary army officer.

Powder House. The sturdy brick magazine built in 1755 was used as an ammunition storehouse in the French-Indian and Revolutionary Wars and in the War of 1812.

Fowler House. The first occupant of the house, built in about 1810, was Samuel Fowler, a prominent industrialist interested in ship-building. Known for its original wallpaper designed by Jean Zuber of France, the house now is a museum. (Open)

DANVERS
MASSACHUSETTS

Witchcraft trials and executions play a prominent part in the early history of Danvers. In 1692, witchcraft delusion broke out in the family of Samuel Parris, minister of the First Village Church. Before the delusion and the trials ended early in the following year with the refusal of a jury to convict accused individuals, 200 persons had been arrested and 20 had been executed, based largely on the testimony of young children. To the public utterances of the Reverend Cotton Mather, who attended one of the executions, was attributed some of the blame for the hysteria that attended the outbreak.

Danvers, which started as a farming area, was settled in 1636, after a grant of 300 acres had been made to John Endicott of Dorchester, England. He called his land Orchard Farm, and it overlooked the Waters River. Henry Bartholomew, Townsend Bishop, and Emmanuel Downing also received early grants. In 1638, families residing in the area, then called Salem Village, were granted, through the Reverend John Philips, the right to establish a village, which by 1650 claimed some 300 able persons as residents.

The first Meeting House, measuring 34 by 28 feet, was built in 1673. A company of militia was formed at about that same time, and a school was established in 1692. In 1752, the town was set off from Salem.

Many local men fought in the French and Indian War between 1760 and 1770, receiving training for later military service, when Danvers men fought in the Battle of Lexington.

Rebecca Nurse or (Nourse) House.
The unusual lean-to house was built, perhaps as early as 1636, on a grant of 300 acres from Governor John Endicott. It was the home of Francis Nurse, husband of Rebecca Nurse, who was accused of witchcraft and hung in 1692 and buried in the yard. It probably is the oldest house in town and is now a museum, charmingly furnished as an early farmhouse. (Open)

Nurse House. An unusual table, whose top folds back to make a chair, is seen in the kitchen.

Nurse House. A narrow stairway of unfinished wood winds up, just inside the doorway.

Nurse House. The front door is studded with closely spaced spikes to discourage the axes of invaders.

Judge Holten House. This was the home of Judge Samuel Holten, who served for five years as a physician in the Continental Army. He was a member of Congress and spent 22 years as a judge of the Court of Common Pleas. It was built in 1670.

Joseph Holten House. The early settler who owned this home, built in 1670, was a voluntary defender of the settlers of Rhode Island in King Philip's War.

Haines House. Easily distinguishable by its large central, dated chimney, the house was built about 1681 by Thomas Haines, step-son of Joseph Holten.

Wadsworth House. Dr. Benjamin Wadsworth, fourth resident pastor of Salem Village Church, built the house with its two entrances in 1785 on land donated by members of the Parish.

Upton Tavern. Walter Smith built this house for his bride in 1710, and in 1791 it became the property of George Upton, who used it as an inn and store. The second-floor ballroom has an arched ceiling.

Page House. Built about 1754, this was the home of Colonel Jeremiah Page. It is said that his wife gave a tea party on the roof before the Revolution to circumvent the popular edict against drinking tea *in* the house. British General Thomas Gage used the dwelling as his office during the Revolution. (Open)

Page House. The splendid desk, under a cornice, is an example of the interesting furniture in the house, which is now a museum of the Danvers Historical Society.

The Lindens. The beautiful stone house was erected in 1754 by Robert Hooper and later was the home of Judge Benejab, formerly of England. Known for its superb paneling and stairway and its long balustrade, the house was the pride of Danvers until it was moved to Washington, D.C. in 1934, piece by piece, where it now sits in the diplomatic and embassy region.

LEXINGTON

MASSACHUSETTS

Until the 19th of April in 1775, Lexington—the "birthplace of the American Revolution"—was a small and peaceful country town. It had been settled in 1640, taking the name of Cambridge Farm. In addition to operating their farms, the people of the new town provided hay and wood to the citizens of nearby Cambridge, of which Lexington was a part until 1691.

The first Meeting House was built in 1713, and Benjamin Estabrook was the first minister. The first schoolhouse was erected on the common in 1715. Roger Herlarkenden built the first house.

Local men participated in the French and Indian Wars, and the survivors formed the nucleus of the militia, to be known as the Minute Men, who met the British troops of General and Governor Thomas Gage.

The governor sent a force of 400 men to seize a supply of muskets and ammunition known to be in Concord, and also to impress the restive colonials with a show of force. News of the British intentions leaked out, however, and after a warning sounded by Paul Revere on his famous ride, some 50 or 60 armed farmers gathered on the green under Captain John Parker.

The Minute Men returned the fire of the British troops, commanded by Major John Pitcairn, after ignoring his order to disperse, but were so vastly outnumbered that Captain Parker ordered his troops to retreat, after leaving eight men dead and nine injured. Later, the Minute Men harassed the British on the way back to Boston after they had accomplished their mission in Concord.

Although there was nothing militarily conclusive about the engagement, the stand of the farmers at Lexington was the beginning of the magnificent colonial resistance that ended in the complete defeat of the British.

After the Revolution, Lexington returned to its peaceful pursuits as an agricultural and residential community.

Milliken House. The original house on this site was burned by the British. This replacement was erected in 1795.

Buckman Tavern. Here was the rallying place of the Minute Men. The old tavern, whose walls show the scars of British bullets, was built in about 1710 by Benjamin Muzzey, who was licensed to keep a public house. At the time of the Battle of Lexington, it was the property of John Buckman, a member of Captain Parker's force. The first village store and the first Post Office were located in the building, which overlooks the Battle Green. (Open)

Buckman Tavern. This is the taproom where the Minute Men gathered to talk and refresh themselves.

Buckman Tavern. The early tavern is noted for its fine old furniture.

Buckman Tavern. Rare china is shown in the crude closet under the exposed beams, flanked by a butter churn and a clock-reel.

Buckman Tavern. A second floor bedroom contains a trundle bed and cradle along with a four-poster bed.

Buckman Tavern. Old relics and kitchen furniture are seen with the kitchen fireplace and its warming bench.

Hancock-Clarke House. The Reverend John Hancock, grandfather of the first signer of the Declaration of Independence, built the first part of the frame house with the simple exterior, in about 1698. It was later the home of the Reverend Jonas Clarke, his successor as pastor of the town church. Young John Hancock, who lived in the house for a period with his grandparents, and Samuel Adams were sleeping there when aroused and warned by Paul Revere after his historic ride from Boston.

Hancock-Clarke House. The fireplace in the parlor is surrounded by Delft tile under the paneled mantel.

Hancock-Clarke House. The old grandfather clock and chest are located in the parlor.

Fiske House. This was the home of Dr. James Fiske, who attended the wounded at the Battle of Lexington and served in the Continental Army as a surgeon throughout the Revolution, after being commissioned by General Washington. The house was built in about 1732.

Jonathan Harrington, Jr., House. Harrington was wounded on the green during the battle and dragged himself to the doorway where he died at his wife's feet. Later the pre-Revolutionary house was the residence of John Augustus, philanthropist and prison reformer. It was also used at one time for the manufacture of wall clocks.

L. Harrington House. This well-shaded house erected in the late 1790's belonged to a relative of Jonathan Harrington, Jr.

Monroe House. Built in about 1729 and facing the green, this was the home of Marrett and Nathan Monroe. The latter was a member of the Minute Men.

Minute Man Statue. The statue shows a Minute Man on guard and is located at the end of Lexington Battle Green, seen to the right.

CONCORD

MASSACHUSETTS

Concord owes its fame to both political and military developments which transpired there in colonial days, and to its later development as a cultural center.

It was settled in about 1635 at a point where the Sudbury and Assabet Rivers meet to form the Concord River. The 12 families who settled there in an Indian village called Muskatequid were led by the Reverend Peter Bulkeley and Simeon Willard, a fur trader. They purchased six square miles of land from the Indians with garments, cloth, hatchets, and knives. After the purchase, the settlers and Indians smoked a pipe of peace, and the name Concord commemorates that friendship, which was never broken.

The First County Convention called to protest the Acts of Parliament was held in Concord in 1774. The First Provincial Congress met there in the same year, and the Second Provincial Congress met in Concord until only a few days before the British attacked in 1775.

Concord was a military supply depot and thus an object of British interest. The Redcoats appeared there in April, 1775, just after the Battle of Lexington and fired on a group of Concord Minute Men while advancing on Old North Bridge. The attackers withdrew after they destroyed the military stores.

So many patriots from Boston took refuge in Concord during the siege of their city that a Boston Town Meeting was held there, and Harvard College conducted classes in Concord when its barracks were converted to military use by the Continental forces.

It was after the war that Concord began to blossom as a cultural center. Among the eminent citizens who became identified with the town were: Ralph Waldo Emerson, Nathaniel Hawthorne, Franklin B. Sanborn, Jane Austin, and Henry David Thoreau, the naturalist. In addition, Amos Bronson Alcott opened his school of philosophy in Concord, and his daughter, Louisa May, wrote her books there, including *Little Women*.

The Wayside. The house, which has been greatly altered, probably consisted of only one room when it was started in the 1600's. The first owner was Nathaniel Ball, followed by Samuel Fletcher, Jr., and Nathaniel Colburn, housewrights; and John Breede, a cordwainer. It eventually was sold to the Alcott family in 1745 and came into the possession of the Hawthorne family a few years later. It was here that Nathaniel Hawthorne wrote his Tanglewood Tales. Flour was stored in the house for emergency use by the patriots in 1774.

Orchard House. Edward Wright, a settler, was the first owner. Bronson Alcott, a later owner, estimated that it was built about 1730, but others believe it to be much older.

Antiquarian House. The charming colonial-style house, which was not constructed until 1928, is a remarkable museum built by the Antiquarian Society to house rare and fascinating relics. (Open)

Antiquarian House. The Green Dining Room, with furniture dating back to 1710–40, has a powdering closet next to the fireplace, in which Chinese porcelain is shown.

Antiquarian House. The fireplace, primitive rocking chair, and settle are in a 17th century room.

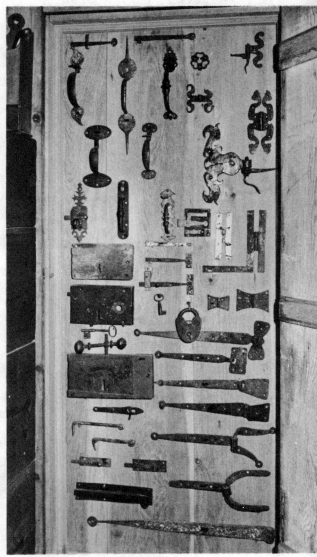

Antiquarian House. The impressive hunt chest also is in the 17th century room.

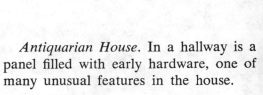

Antiquarian House. In a hallway is a panel filled with early hardware, one of many unusual features in the house.

Antiquarian House. Also in the hall-way is a seldom seen latch string and its wooden latch on an old pine door.

Antiquarian House. Old furniture and a paneled wall with a Queen Anne fireplace can be seen in one of the parlors.

Brown House. Peter Bulkeley, a distinguished citizen and original settler and a colonial emmisary to London, built the house for his bride at about the time of their wedding between 1666–1668. It was set on fire by the British but fortunately was saved. Later it was the home of Reuben Brown, a saddler, who carried the news of the Battle of Lexington to Concord.

Wright Tavern. At the time of the Battle of Concord, British Major Pitcairn had his headquarters in the tavern erected in about 1747.

Colonial Inn. The old part of the inn, formed by joining three houses, was built about 1770. The taproom has its original fittings and Revolutionary relics.

The Old Manse. The Reverend William Emerson, militant preacher and grandfather of Ralph Waldo Emerson, built the large, dark gray, clapboard house with its lean-to in 1765. Nathaniel Hawthorne later lived there.

Minute Man Statue. In making the statue, located near the Old North Bridge, Daniel C. French, the sculptor, is said to have used a statue of Apollo Belvedere as a model.

DEDHAM

MASSACHUSETTS

That the men who settled Dedham in 1635 were seeking social and economic advancement rather than religious liberty is suggested in the town covenant, which announces their purpose of being "a loving and comfortable society."

Blessed with fruitful soil, the town located just south of Boston but away from the ocean became a prosperous farming center until industry was attracted there years later.

To minimize damage by fire, a town ordinance required each householder to provide and maintain a good and sufficient ladder, long enough to reach the chimney of the house, and an annual inspection was made by a chimney-viewer. Another early ordinance forbade the use of clapboards for fear the Indians would place fire brands under the boards.

Dedham was barely touched by the Indian wars or by later conflicts, and little of note transpired until 1818, when a historic decision of the Supreme Court of Massachusetts gave the right to elect ministers to the Dedham Parish, rather than the church fellowship, thus paving the way for the rise of Unitarianism in the State.

In the old Woodward Tavern, long gone from the scene, was held the Suffolk Convention for the drafting of the Suffolk Resolves, thereby lighting the match, according to a tablet on the courthouse, that "kindled the mighty conflagration of the American Revolution."

Dedham became more widely known, at least temporarily, in 1921 when it was the scene of the controversial Sacco-Vanzetti trial.

Fairbanks House. The old brown house with its many additions and sagging roofline was erected by Jonathan Fairbanks in about 1636 and contains oak timbers said to have been brought from England. The entrance hall which is only eight feet long and three and a quarter feet wide has doors leading to five rooms. The aging farmhouse is 75 feet long. Near the front entrance are eight windows, no two of them identical. The house remained in the same family for three centuries. (Open)

Fairbanks House. The old stone well with its long pole-sweep is prominent in the front yard.

Fairbanks House. Aged wood walls adjoin the fireplace. The hinged arm seen in the upper left is a blanket warmer, used in the days of unheated bedrooms.

Powder House. The little brick powder magazine was built in 1766 on a high outcropping of rock.

Haven House. Judge Samuel Haven built the large white, three-story house in 1795. It is now a community center. (Open)

First Church. The beautiful edifice constructed in 1768 has round-topped doors under the pediment. (Open)

Congregational Church. This church, which faces the earlier First Church, was built in 1819 by dissenting members of the latter. Modest in appearance at first glance, it has high-backed pews. (Open)

Dexter House. Samuel Dexter, son of the Reverend Samuel Dexter, who was a colonial merchant and member of the Provincial Congress, built the large square house in about 1762. Young Dexter made a small fortune in Boston by the age of 36 and "retired" to Dedham. Located behind a tall hedge, the house was the showplace of the old town. George Washington spent a night there.

Dexter House. The dining room is richly furnished with family heirlooms, including the handsome bow-front sideboard.

Dexter House. The stairway is distinctive for its bold carving.

Dexter House. Fine old wallpaper graces the large drawing room furnished with splendid antiques.

PLYMOUTH
MASSACHUSETTS

Plymouth was founded by the Pilgrims from the *Mayflower,* which had been destined for Virginia but was blown off its course. Among the small group of men who landed on that historic day at Plymouth Rock in 1620 were Captain Miles Standish and future governors of the colony, John Carver and William Bradford.

A bountiful harvest after the first winter of illness, hardship, and discouragement during which almost half of the colony perished, led to the celebration of Thanksgiving Day.

The best picture of the early days at Plymouth was given in a letter written to Holland in 1627 by a Dutchman, who said in part:

"The houses are constructed of hewn planks, with gardens also enclosed behind and at the sides with hewn planks, so that their houses and court-yards are arranged in very good order, with a stockade against sudden attack; and at the ends of the street are three wooden gates. In the centre, on the cross street, stands the Governor's house, before which is a square enclosure, upon which four pateros are mounted, so as to flank along the street.

"Upon the hill they have a large square house, with a flat roof, made of thick sawn planks, stayed with oak beams, upon the top of which they have six cannons, which shoot balls of four and five pounds, and command the surrounding country. The lower part they use for their church, where they preach on Sundays and the usual holidays. They assemble by beat of drum, each with his musket or firelock, in front of the Captain's door; they have their cloaks on, and place themselves in order, three abreast, and are led by a sergeant without beat of drum. . . . Thus are they constantly on their guard, night and day."

Antiquarian House. Major William Hammatt built the house in 1809. It has a long front yard facing Cape Cod Bay. Now the headquarters of the Plymouth Antiquarian Society, the house is a museum furnished like a prosperous Plymouth home of the early 1800's. (Open)

Antiquarian House. Mannequins in period dress add interest to the well-furnished drawing room.

Antiquarian House. Old china and household utensils are displayed near the kitchen.

119

Antiquarian House. This is the music room.

Antiquarian House. The desk with the ball feet and the chair are placed in a corner of a first-floor parlor.

Plackett House. Built about 1722, this was the home of Consider Howland, grandson of John Howland, a *Mayflower* passenger. At one time it was a school run by Tabitha Plackett, who, it is said, punished her pupils by placing skeins of yarn around beneath their arms and hanging the "rascals" up on hooks.

Winslow House. Edward Winslow, grandson of Governor Edward Winslow of the Mayflower Company and brother of General John Winslow, erected this spendid house in 1754. It was greatly enlarged in 1800. Ralph Waldo Emerson was married there. It now is the headquarters of the National Society of Mayflower Descendants. (Open)

121

Spooner House. Another beautifully furnished house of the Antiquarian Society, Spooner House was built in about 1742 by Josiah Rider and was the home of five generations of Spooners, starting in 1763. At one time, it was a chocolate shop. (Open)

Spooner House. The tiled fireplace and tall grandfather clock are in a first-floor parlor.

Spooner House. The entrance hall is narrow and short.

Leonard House. The Reverend Nathaniel Leonard, pastor of the First Church, built this center-chimney house in about 1734.

Old Town House. Erected in 1749 to serve as the courthouse, the building later became the Town Hall.

Bonum House. This faded frame house built in 1677 was the home of George Bonum.

Sparrow House. Now a pottery workshop, the old part of the house, on the left, with its narrow casement windows and diamond-shaped panes, was built about 1640. (Open)

Harlow House. Built of great beams taken from an early Plymouth fort, the house was erected in about 1677 on part of the original common. It was the home of Sergeant William Harlow, who presumably served in the French and Indian War and later was a surveyor, assessor, excise officer, inspector of taverns, and selectman. It had become a two-family tenement before its purchase in 1920 by the Antiquarian Society. The house is shaded by an enormous silver-leaf poplar. (Open)

Harlow House. This is the drain through which waste water was discharged from the kitchen.

Kendall-Holmes House. William Harlow built this homestead house in 1649 for his bride, who was the granddaughter of a Mayflower passenger. It still holds much of its original furniture.

OLD DEERFIELD

MASSACHUSETTS

Twice a virtual ghost town, Old Deerfield today is strictly a tiny school and museum town situated near the Connecticut River on land granted to the town of Dedham in 1663.

The site was laid out in 1665, but no one from Dedham came until Samuel Hindsdell squatted there in 1669. Samson Frary and others joined him in 1672, when Old Deerfield was the northwestern frontier of the colonies.

The little town had 125 people in 1675, and things were prospering in a modest way, until the outbreak of King Philip's War saw the beginning of a series of attacks that kept the townspeople in a state of continuous terror for 30 years.

The Bloody Brook Massacre of 1675 emptied the town. The garrison was withdrawn, and the people scattered among the nearby villages. For the next seven years, the town's houses remained empty, but in 1678 the General Court gave the former residents permission to return, and the town was re-established in 1682. John Williams, who became Old Deerfield's most illustrious citizen, was induced to take over the church in 1686.

Then, during Queen Anne's War in 1704, came the terrible Deerfield Raid in which half the town was burned, 49 people were killed, and 110 persons, including Williams, were taken captive to Canada.

Rehabilitation was slow and ineffectual after the raid, and not until the first of the schools was founded did Old Deerfield again begin to come alive.

Ashley House. An early occupant of the house was the Reverend Jonathan Ashley, aggressive preacher, incorrigible loyalist, and militant Tory. Built prior to 1732, the house contains 17th and 18th century furniture. Before it was restored, the house was used as a tobacco barn. (Open)

Ashley House. Intricate carving surrounds the front entrance with its paneled door and small bull's-eye windows.

Sheldon-Hawks House. The weatherbeaten house, owned by the Sheldon family for two centuries, was erected in about 1743. It has fine interior paneling and a rear stairway with a dual approach. The furnishings include old family pieces and a sewing room with old models, dresses, and fabrics. (Open)

Sheldon-Hawks House. Here is another elaborate entrance.

Parker & Russell House. The Clesson family built the house in 1814. It has been moved twice but is now back at its original site. Isaac Parker, an early resident, was a silversmith, and John Russell was his apprentice. (Open)

Stebbins House. The brick house was completed in 1790 for Asa Stebbins, son of a wealthy land owner. During the Revolution, Stebbins is said to have dealt with both sides. The house contains Hepplewhite and Sheraton furniture, and portraits by Gilbert Stuart, John Greenwood, and others. The south parlor has a rare plaster ceiling. (Open)

Hall Tavern. Built in the 1700's as a tavern at Charlemont on the Mohawk Trail, the long tavern has a pewterer's room, wallpaper shop, and fabric room. It also has a ballroom with a vaulted ceiling. (Open)

Frary House. Samson Frary started to build the large frame house in 1689. It was one of the few residences to escape burning in the Indian raids, during which Frary was killed. The house, which was a center of Whig activity during the Revolution, has a beautiful ballroom with a fiddler's balcony. (Open)

Frary House. This entrance is unusual for Deerfield, in that it is covered by a porch.

Wells-Thorn House. Here was the home of Ebeneezer Wells, farmer, tavern keeper, and merchant. The oldest part was built in about 1717, a later part in 1751. On the second floor is the law office of Hezekiah W. Strong, which still is equipped with his furniture of about 1800. (Open)

Dwight-Barnard House. In 1754 Josiah Dwight built the house in Springfield, Massachusetts, from where it was moved. Inside are a large kitchen which also served as a living room, excellent portraits, and an old doctor's office. (Open)

Wilson House. The house, erected in 1816, was moved five times before being returned to its original location. It started as a print shop and was later used by a grocer and a cabinet maker. (Open)

NORTHAMPTON

MASSACHUSETTS

It was in Northampton that the Reverend Jonathan Edwards, a Puritan divine, gained his reputation as a powerful preacher and later became an inspired leader of America's first great revival movement in 1740. So great was the frenzy of religious hysteria that people began to fall into spellbound trances and to see visions, as they were convulsed with the fear of impending hellfire, real or imagined.

Eventually, dissention in his congregation led to Edwards' dismissal after 23 years in Northampton, and he went to Stockbridge, Massachusetts, where he became a missionary to the Indians. It was there that he wrote his notable philosophical treatise, "On the Freedom of the Will."

The town was settled in 1654 after a group of men in Connecticut petitioned the General Court for permission to establish a town north of Hartford. Each of the early settlers received four acres of land, plus a generous portion of meadow.

Northampton was not greatly bothered by Indian attacks in the early days. The Nonotuck Tribe had left the area when the French and Indian Wars began, but other tribes harassed the settlers when King Philip's War started.

After the Revolution, the inhabitants of the town, led by a preacher named Sam Ely, rose in rebellion and stormed the courthouse to protest foreclosure of their farms. That was in 1782. Again in 1786, near the end of Shay's Rebellion intended to obtain legislative relief for owners of farms, a crowd of angry citizens descended on the court to keep it from holding sessions and taking hostile action.

The founding of Smith College in 1875 was another notable event in Northampton history.

Smith Homestead. Erected in 1790, this was the birthplace of Sophia Smith, founder of Smith College. It was purchased and furnished by alumnae of the college.

Parsons House. Cornet Joseph Parsons, an early settler, built the house in 1655–58. It has been furnished as a museum with early local furniture by the local historical society. (Open)

Parsons House. Old utensils and furniture are seen in the wood-paneled kitchen.

Parsons House. The cutaway wall section shows how split saplings covered with plaster were used in early partitions before laths came into use.

Parsons House. Walls of the house are framed with sturdy timbers covered with extremely wide pine boards.

Damon House. Another Historical Society House furnished with relics and Jenny Lind articles, this low-roofed framed dwelling was built in 1812 by Isaac Damon. (Open)

Wiggins Tavern. The three-story brick building erected in 1786 is now part of a modern inn. (Open)

Sessions House. Lieutenant Jonathan Hunt built the house in 1700. It is regarded as the most beautiful early American house in the area. Now the property of Smith College, it is said to have a secret stairway.

Porter-Phelps-Huntington House. Captain Moses Porter built the massive, rambling house with its wide single shutters in 1752. It has had no structural changes since 1799, and its contents have been kept intact for two centuries, providing an unusual and impressive collection of valuable antiques. Private family papers, collected by ten successive generations, including deeds, wills, bills, diaries, and so forth, date from 1697. (Open)

HADLEY
MASSACHUSETTS

A most interesting event in the history of Hadley was the experience of Mary Webster who, in 1683, was accused of bewitching and murdering Deacon Philip Smith and was then hung until nearly dead, cut down, and buried in the snow. Somehow she survived, and a few years later she died of natural causes.

The town on the Connecticut River, across from Northampton, was settled in 1659 and named for Hadleigh, England, by John Webster and the Reverend John Russell. They had left Connecticut because of religious controversies.

A marker identifies the site of the home in which the Reverend Russell protected and hid two fugitives for 15 years. They were Edmund Whalley and William Goffe, members of the High Court of Justice that condemned King Charles I of England to death. The two men fled to America after the monarchy was restored, and Charles II had issued warrants for the arrest of his father's "murderers."

After landing in Boston in 1660 and finding themselves hunted by royal officers, the men fled west and finally arrived in Hadley in 1664. Whalley died in the Russell home.

As early as 1663, the town voted to give 20 pounds a year for three years for a schoolmaster to teach the children, and Caleb Watson was the first master. The school met in a house provided by Goodman Ware until 1698, when the town built a schoolhouse measuring 25 by 18 feet, located by error in the middle of a street.

In 1814, Hadley was the birthplace of Major General "Fighting Joe" Hooker of Civil War fame.

Porter-Phelps-Huntington House.
Scarred old paneling surrounds the fireplace. In the foreground is a foot warmer.

Porter-Phelps-Huntington House
Small drawers are built between the folding inside shutters, which swing above the window seats.

Porter-Phelps-Huntington House. A desk rests on a dropleaf table in an upstairs room once used as an office.

Eleazar Porter House. This house built in 1713, the oldest in town, was the home of the Eleazar Porter family. The elaborate two-leaf, paneled front door is surmounted by a high scroll. One of the rooms was used as a Court Council room.

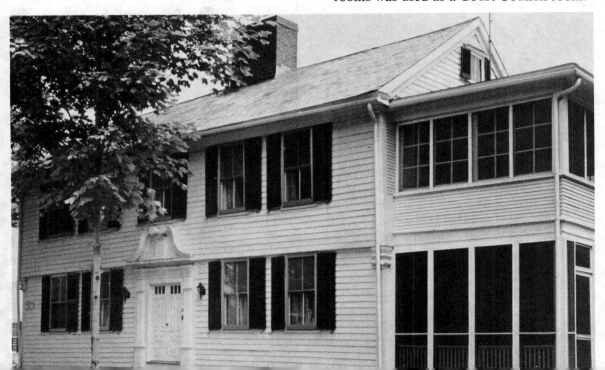

141

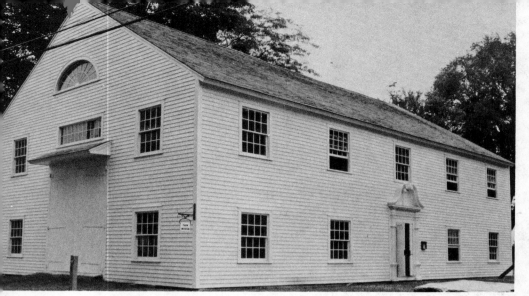

Farm Museum. The large structure, which now houses a museum, was built in 1782 and moved into town from an outlying farm. The front entrance, unusually elaborate for a barn, appears to be identical in design with that of the Eleazar Porter house. (Open)

Congregational Church. Built in 1808, the church with the tall spire houses a communion service presented to the parish in 1724 and a weathercock that came from England in 1752. It cost $8413 to build and the sale of 78 pews brought in $7031. The bell cost $200. (Open)

Allen Tavern. The large old inn, built in the 1700's, is notable for the rows of seven windows in its main facade and the gable over the large door.

EAST GREENWICH

RHODE ISLAND

This town on the west side of Narragansett Bay had two especially prominent citizens in its early days, both soldiers. General Nathanael Greene, who started in the Revolutionary War as a private in the Kentish Guards and shortly afterward was commissioned a Brigadier General in the Continental Army, is regarded locally as the most brilliant soldier of the war, after George Washington.

The other eminent soldier was General James Mitchell Varnum, a lawyer before and after the war, who later became a U.S. judge in the Northwest Territory.

The town was founded in 1677, following the decision of the Rhode Island General Assembly to lay out a tract of 5000 acres there, including 50 home lots. The latter were granted to veterans of King Philip's War.

Blessed with a good harbor, the new town shared its activity between agriculture and fishing. Its waterfront boasted a shipyard, ropewalk, and later a whale oil works. Using the port were whaling ships and coastal and West Indies trading schooners. A pottery works was another early venture.

In 1686, a group of educated Huguenots bought a tract of land but, after a few years, were squeezed out as squatters. Their number included glovemakers, lace-makers, and tanners, and they brought fruit trees and grape vines with them.

In 1700, the downtown district was divided into quarter-acre lots by a group called the Proprietors, and the lots were assigned to the townsfolk by drawing numbers from hats.

As early as 1767, the General Assembly, sitting in the Kent County Courthouse in East Greenwich, expressed the principles of liberty for which so many were soon to lose their lives. This early expression prompts the claim that the venerable courthouse is the "Independence Hall of Rhode Island."

White Swan Tavern. Now a private home, the tavern was erected in the late 1700's on the Old Post Road.

Greene House. Once the home of U.S. Senator Albert C. Greene, the house in the heart of town was built in 1724. The first bank in East Greenwich was formerly located in the left end.

Kent County Courthouse. Situated on a rise, the three-and-a-half story structure was built in 1750, and the exterior has remained unchanged through the years. The convention for the framing of Rhode Island's Constitution met here in 1842.

Captain John Congdon House. Whether the house was built in 1711 as the date on the chimney suggests or in 1750 as some authorities believe, it is a well-preserved house. James Miller had a silversmith shop there, and Nathan Miller, another occupant, was a bayonet maker.

Captain John Congdon House. The unusual arch and broad beams are seen in the parlor.

Eldredge House. The large frame house, which stands well above the street and now shows its age, was built in 1757 by James Reynolds. It later was sold, along with a bake shop, to Nathan Greene, a tanner. When Dr. Charles Eldredge bought the house, he located his office there.

Windmill House. The house takes its name from the hexagonal structure that once supported a windmill. It was built in about 1800 and was later bought by the poet Henry Wadsworth Longfellow. He moved the windmill there to serve as a study for his friend, Dr. George Washington Greene, a diplomat and historian, who was the grandson of General Nathanael Greene.

Varnum House. This graceful mansion, the home of General Varnum, was built in 1773 on an eminence overlooking Narragansett Bay. A spacious central hall runs through the house on both floors, and every room has a fireplace. Other prominent men lived in it after General Varnum's death. The house is furnished with notable pieces of the Revolutionary period. (Open)

Varnum House. The desk is in the General's combination library and law office.

Varnum House. The mantel over the kitchen fireplace has unusual recessed shelves.

Varnum House. The fireplace in the drawing room is surrounded with beautiful tile.

149

Varnum House. A delicate cornice and broken pediment over the fireplace add interest to the dining room.

STONINGTON
CONNECTICUT

Situated on a long point that juts out into the Atlantic Ocean near the Rhode Island line, Stonington twice was the object of a British attack from the sea. The first attack by a foraging party in 1775 was repulsed by the militia without serious loss. Then, in 1814, five British ships with a total of 140 guns bombarded the town for three days. The militia, armed with only two small cannons, not only defended the town successfully, but drove the British off with one ship badly damaged and 94 casualties, against only two casualties among the defenders.

Stonington, which was called both Pawcatuck and Mistack by the Narragansett Indians who lived there, was settled in 1649 by William Cheeseborough and a group from Plymouth. There were some early battles against the Indians but the colonists experienced few casualties.

In its early days the town was such an active ship-building center that it gained the name of "Nursery for seamen." Its merchant vessels and whaling ships sailed the seven seas in search of profitable cargo. Ship-building continued until the Civil War, after which it subsided as steamships began to take over.

Two local brothers gained prominence by serving under John Paul Jones at the time of the Revolution. Captain Edward Fanning was a midshipman under Jones, and his brother, Nathaniel, was a maintopman on Jones' *Bonhomme Richard* and took part in the historic fight against the *Serapis*.

Denison House. The densely shaded frame house built in 1720 was the home of Edward Denison. It later became a tavern. It has a ballroom and interesting corner cupboards. A daughter-in-law of the owner is said to have drowned herself in a nearby well.

Palmer House. This home of Dudley Palmer, built in 1765, became a whaling museum.

Amos Palmer House. Recognized by its high basement, the house built in 1787 was badly damaged in the British bombardment of 1814. It was the boyhood home of James A.M. Whistler, who built a railroad to Providence. The interior contains excellent paneling and mantels.

Edward Fanning House. Known for its quaint interior woodwork, the house was started in about 1720. One-time midshipman Fanning was its owner.

Edward Fanning House. The narrow, winding stairway rises from just inside the front door.

Edward Fanning House. The fireplace in the parlor is surrounded by dignified hand-carved paneling.

Edward Fanning House. This is a house of numerous paneled fireplaces.

Edward Fanning House. Hanging around the old kitchen fireplace are numerous griddles, pans, and other relics.

Gilbert Fanning House. This formerly was a tavern, which was formed by joining three houses together. The houses were built between 1720–1750.

Pendleton House. Captain William Pendleton, master mariner and ship owner, lived in the house built in the late 1700's.

Ash House. A ropemaker, Thomas Ash, owned this little house, erected in about 1700.

Cannon Square. In this tiny green overlooking the waterfront are the two cannons used in the succesful defense of Stonington during the British attack of 1814.

WINDSOR

CONNECTICUT

Like the Pilgrims at Plymouth from whence they came, the early settlers of Windsor had a terrifying first winter of hardship, bitter cold, and short rations. Many of them left and were picked up at Saybrook by a relief ship that returned them to Massachusetts.

The settlers of the town at the mouth of the Farmington River arrived in 1633 under the leadership of Captain William Holmes. On the way up the Connecticut River, they were ordered to stop and surrender by the commander of a Dutch fort at Hartford, but they kept on going. When the Dutch later sent a force to drive the new settlers away, the palisades which had been set up for protection against both the Dutch and the Indians looked too strong and the would-be attackers withdrew.

Puritans from Dorchester joined the new settlement in 1635 and then a third group of colonists arrived from England led by Sir Richard Saltonstall.

The Indians called the location Matianuck, and it was known as Dorchester until it took the name Windsor in 1637.

The Indians hadn't made any serious trouble at Windsor, but fearful of attack after a raid on Wethersfield, Captain John Mason led a group of townsmen who burned out an Indian village at Mystic. The town then remained relatively untroubled until King Philip's War began, and farmers fled there from Simsburg for protection.

Among the prominent men of early times was Sergeant David Bissell, who was cited by George Washington in 1783 and received the then rarely given Purple Heart. Windsor was also the home of Oliver Ellsworth, appointed Chief Justice of the U. S. Supreme Court by Washington and later sent to Paris where he negotiated a treaty with Napoleon. Roger Wolcott, governor of Connecticut, also lived there.

Tobacco-growing quickly became the major occupation of the farmers in the Windsor area, and it still is an important crop there today.

Ellsworth Homestead. This was the home of Oliver Ellsworth, member of the Continental Congress, U.S. Senator, Minister to France, and Chief Justice. The drawing room of the central-hall house built in 1740 is paneled in mahogany and contains tapestry presented by Napoleon following the negotiation of the treaty with France by Ellsworth. Washington, Lafayette, and John Adams all were visitors to the homestead. (Open)

Ellsworth House. This modest frame house was built in 1807 and was presented by Oliver Ellsworth to his son, Martin.

Stoughton House. An early owner of this frame house with the central chimney, and erected in 1735, was Captain Sam Stoughton.

Chaffee House. One of the oldest brick houses in the area, this home of Hezekiah Chaffee was built in 1765 and later became a school.

Fyler House. The early section of this house was built in about 1640 on land given to Lieutenant Walter Fyler for his valiant service in the Pequot War in 1637. After 123 years in the Fyler family, it was purchased by Nathaniel Howward, a sea captain. Later it became the first Post Office in town and also saw use as a store. The house is now a fascinating museum of the Windsor Historical Society. (Open)

Fyler House. For such an old house, it has an elaborate entrance and a paneled door of unusual design.

Fyler House. The plain battened inner design of the same door contrasts with the door's outer splendor.

Fyler House. Under the old table the pronounced sag in the floor of the keeping room is readily seen.

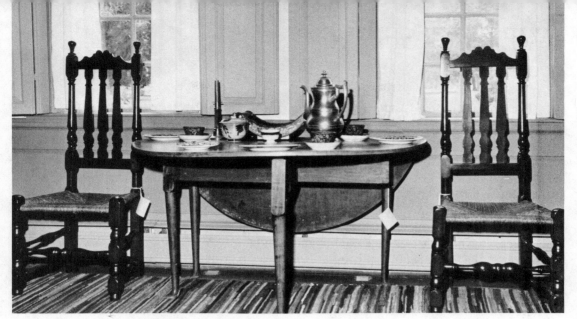

Fyler House. Paneled folding shutters and old furniture can be seen in the parlor.

Fyler House. In a store room on the second floor, the primitive roof and wall construction of wide boards and tree trunks is visible.

163

WETHERSFIELD

CONNECTICUT

The town on the Connecticut River prides itself on being the scene of the first demonstration of the American people for independence, when in 1640 the townsmen held an election in defiance of the Royal Courts. When a fine of five pounds was assessed against the town for its indiscretion, it refused to pay.

Later, during the Stamp Act controversy, the independent people of Wethersfield forced Jared Ingersoll, a newly appointed tax collector, to march under escort to Hartford to resign his office.

John Oldham, of Watertown, Massachusetts, and a party of ten men were the town's first settlers, arriving in 1635. The Indian name for the region was Pyquag.

From the beginning, the Pequot Indians were eager to regain their traditional hunting grounds which the white men had pre-empted. They kept the settlers in a state of apprehension, and in 1637 the massacre of six men and three women and the abduction of two girls precipitated the Pequot War.

In the 1700's, during the witchcraft hysteria, a woman named Mary Johnson was hanged after confessing familiarity with the devil, and John Carrington and his wife were both convicted of witchcraft and hanged.

John Oldham, probably the first owner and master of a ship built in Wethersfield, was murdered by Indians near Block Island. Thomas Deming, a ship's carpenter, built the first shipyard in Wethersfield in 1648.

The first commercial ship built in Connecticut—the *Tryall*—was launched there in 1649, and with its early ships Wethersfield developed a large export trade in onions and pipe staves. Wethersfield was authorized to export 30,000 staves annually. The staves were either shipped to the West Indies, where they were used in pipes and hogsheads and then returned full of rum, molasses, and sugar, or else were used locally in casks in which salt-beef, pork, and fish were shipped to the Indies.

Buttolph-Williams House. A trestle-foot, gateleg table, and antique chairs rest under the timbered ceiling in the "greate kitchin."

Buttolph-Williams House. A close-up of the exterior shows the overhang and the plain entrance door of vertical boards.

Buttolph-Williams House. The house, which has its original unpainted exterior, was built in about 1692 by David Buttolph. A few years later, it came into the possession of Benjamin Beldon, who was licensed to keep a tavern. The house was then sold to Daniel Williams, whose family occupied it for many years. It contains an outstanding collection of early antiques and relics and is operated as a museum by the Antiquarian & Landmarks Society of Connecticut. (Open)

Buttolph-Williams House. A rare, half-circle settle stands close by the old fireplace and its early utensils.

Buttolph-Williams House. Also in the kitchen is a display of pewter and other early Americana.

Buttolph-Williams House. The old kitchen is a treasure-chest of rare furniture, including twin highchairs.

Buttolph-Williams House. A splendid old Hartford chest stands between graceful matching chairs.

Buttolph-Williams House. The bedrooms are also interestingly furnished under beamed ceilings.

Congregational Church. The tall brick church with the colonial steeple was erected in about 1761, the third church to occupy the site.

Deane House. The Connecticut Society of Colonial Dames has undertaken the restoration of the frame house built in 1766. It was the home of Silas Deane, a member of the Continental Congress, and was the place where in 1775 the capture of Fort Ticonderoga was conceived by a group of local men. The paneled doorway is greatly admired.

Webb House. A central hall runs through to the garden in this house built by James Webb in about 1752. Here, in the south parlor in 1781, George Washington and the Comte de Rochambeau planned the campaign which led to the Battle of Yorktown and the surrender of Cornwallis. Original imported wallpaper is still preserved in the room where Washington slept. The house contains many rare items that give an authentic picture of early 18th century living. The Colonial Dames also maintain this home. (Open)

The Academy. The brick structure erected in about 1801 is where the Reverend Joseph Emerson conducted a seminary. It later became a public school and then a town hall and library.

Ashbul Wright House. This was the home of the Reverend Mr. Emerson, a pioneer in advanced education for women. It was built in about 1786.

Latimer House. Though now clap-
boarded, the house was built in 1690
with outer walls of rough vertical planks
two and a half inches thick. This was
one of six houses ordered to be fortified
against Indian attack in 1703. It was
the home of Captain Jack Latimer, con-
stable, collector, and surveyor of highways, and son of a settler who came in
1635.

FARMINGTON
CONNECTICUT

Always a quiet and peaceful town, Farmington has a monument to the Comte de Rochambeau, the French general, who commanded forces sent by his country to help the Continental Army during the Revolution. Prior to their participation in the siege and victory at Yorktown in 1781, his troops had an encampment near Farmington.

Though it started as a farming community, after the Revolution it became the seat of numerous small industries, which turned out linens, hats, leather goods, muskets, and butter. It also had bootmakers, clockmakers, carriage and cabinet makers, and smiths dealing in silver, gold, and tin, whose output was marketed in the territory to the south by Yankee peddlers who carried packs on their backs or rode on horseback or in wagons. There is no record that Farmington was the source of the wooden nutmegs and oakleaf tobacco that some of the less scrupulous peddlers from Connecticut were accused of selling in the old days.

The town was settled in 1640 by col-onists from Hartford. They were led by Captain John Mason, the Indian fighter, who had explored the region when it was inhabited by the Tunxis Indians. After the massacre at Deerfield, the town's citizens voted to fortify seven houses. At one time an agreement was reached with friendly Indians whereby the settlers would plough for the Indians who, in turn, could cut wood and sell corn and hides to the settlers.

The early, rough log huts had wooden chimneys with a clay lining and here, as elsewhere, ladders were required and chimney viewers inspected chimneys regularly to guard against fire.

Women often came to church on pillions and there were "sabba-day" or Sabbath houses where fresh coals could be obtained for foot warmers and where members of the Congregation could obtain rest and comfort when services and sermons were overlong.

The original town, which once covered 165 square miles, eventually was divided into nine separate towns.

172

Stanley-Whitman House. The oven is in the back of the old kitchen fireplace, which has a massive wooden lintel.

Stanley-Whitman House. The old built-in corner cupboard sits beneath exposed beams in the kitchen.

Stanley-Whitman House. This unstained clapboard saltbox, with its overhang and narrow casement windows, was built about 1660. Two of its doors are studded. It has been carefully restored and now serves as a fine museum. (Open)

Stanley-Whitman House. An intriguing
display of old-time feminine attire is seen
in a bedroom.

Judd House. Adjoining the Thompson
house is the one-time home of Benjamin
Judd, dating from 1697.

174

Whitman Tavern. Captain Joseph Woodruff, master builder, erected the house in 1786 on a nearby location. It became a shop for journeymen shoe-makers, later it was a tavern, and then served as a village library.

Elm Tree Inn. The oldest portion of the present large inn was built in 1665 by Philip (Phinehas) Lewis to serve as a tavern.

Thompsan House. Once the home of James Thompson, the center-chimney house was erected in 1739.

Congregational Church. The builder of Whitman Tavern was the architect for the church with its tall slender spire and open belfry. It was erected in 1771. (Open)

101 Main Street. Another of the town's oldest buildings, this frame house was started in 1690.

LITCHFIELD

CONNECTICUT

The town's land was bought from the Indians in 1715–16 for 15 pounds, but was not settled until 1720 when Captain Jacob Griswold and others arrived. Captain Griswold later was taken captive by the Indians but he managed to escape.

Well before its development as a residential community of great charm, Litchfield was an outpost and trading center. It also had a growing number of farms and numerous small mills on nearby streams.

At the outbreak of the Revolution, during which it was an important military supply depot, men from Litchfield were sent to Bunker Hill as reinforcements. Aaron Burr, who had been living there, enlisted and served in Benedict Arnold's expedition to Canada.

Other noted citizens included Oliver Wolcott, who was a member of the Continental Congress, a signer of the Declaration of Independence, and later Governor of Connecticut.

Another was Tapping Reeve, who founded in Litchfield the first law school in America. Reeve was among the first to champion the legal rights of married women and imbued his students with a strong desire to defend the oppressed. Among the graduates of his school were a Vice-President of the United States, five cabinet members, five diplomats, 17 U.S. Senators, 53 members of the House of Representatives, three Associate Justices of the U.S. Supreme Court, and ten state governors.

In addition, there was Julius Deming, a successful merchant and ship owner, who came to Litchfield from North Lyme down on the coast and started the Litchfield China Trading Company, which for 14 years traded with the orient using the port of New Haven. Incoming cargoes were hauled to the trading center in Litchfield—by ox teams.

Other famous people born there include Ethan Allen, Harriett Beecher Stowe, and her brother Henry Ward Beecher. Litchfield also was the home of the first "Female Academy" in America, founded by Miss Sally Pierce.

Allen House. John Allen, a lawyer and member of Congress, started the house in 1797. It has unusually high ceilings and doorways, perhaps because Allen was a tall man.

Sheldon's Tavern. Tall trees block the view of a Palladian window on the front of the house built in 1760 by Elisha Sheldon. His son later converted it into the first tavern in town, and George Washington was a guest there. Later it became the home of Judge Gould.

Tallmadge House. Thomas Sheldon erected the house in about 1775. It is believed that Colonel Benjamin Tallmadge, aide-de-camp to George Washington, added the unusual two-story porticos at each end of the house sometime later. William Franklin, the Royal Governor of New Jersey and son of Benjamin Franklin, was held as a hostage in the house during the Revolution, and George Washington once held a reception there.

Deming House. The house with the handsome facade was built in 1793 under the direction of William Spratt, an early architect. It was the home of Julius Deming, the china trader. His company bought 200 horses to improve the stock of this country.

The Corner House. Charles Butler built the long house in 1792. It is admired for its interesting doorway and tall portico.

The Apothecary Shop. The little store-building was erected in 1781 by Dr. Reuben Smith for use as a shop and office. It is now a book store. (Open)

Samuel Seymour House. Now the Episcopal Rectory, this is where John C. Calhoun, later Vice-President of the United States, is said to have lived while he was a law student in Litchfield. The house, built in 1784, has an overhang on two floors.

Tapping Reeve House. This was the home of Judge Reeve, who started the country's first law school. It is magnificently furnished and is maintained as a museum by the Litchfield Historical Society. Some of its outstanding furnishings were once loaned to Yale University and have been returned to the house. Judge Reeve married Sally Burr, sister of Aaron Burr, who was one of Reeve's first students. The house was built in 1773–4 by Moses Seymour at about the same time the school started. (Open)

Tapping Reeve House. A fine portrait of George Washington hangs on the handsome overmantel.

182

Tapping Reeve House. The side chairs and drop-leaf table are examples of the splendid furniture seen in the parlor.

Tapping Reeve House. Fine paneling and old furniture, including the lowboy and circular corner cupboard, are on the first floor.

Tapping Reeve House. The desk probably was used by Judge Reeve.

Tapping Reeve House. The grandfather clock and desk are placed at the head of the stairway on the second floor.

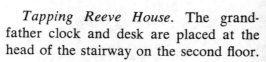

Tapping Reeve House. A graceful old four-poster is in one of the bedrooms.

The Law School. This little building, located in a formal garden near the house, is where Judge Reeve's law classes met, starting in 1784.

Oliver Wolcott, Sr., House. This was the home of the elder Wolcott. It was built in 1753 and occupied by his direct descendants for 200 years. Behind this house, a statue of George III, which had been torn from its pedestal in New York City and brought to Litchfield by ox cart, was melted into 42,088 bullets by loyal ladies of the town for use by the Continental Army.

Oliver Wolcott, Jr., House. Eliza Wadsworth built the house in 1799. On the second floor, it had a large paneled ballroom, which later was divided in two. A row of dormers in front and a small porch have been removed. It was the home of the younger Wolcott, who succeeded Alexander Hamilton as Secretary of the Treasury and who later succeeded his father as Governor of Connecticut. The house is being refurbished by the Litchfield Historical Society to which it recently was donated by a member of the Wadsworth family.

The Village Green. With its monument and Revolutionary cannon, the green divides the town, north and south.

WOODBURY

CONNECTICUT

Chief Pomperaug, for whom its river is named and who is said to be buried beneath a boulder near Main Street, was the proprietor of the Woodbury region when it was first settled by white men in 1672.

During the Revolution, Woodbury seethed with patriotism, and many of its residents served with Ethan Allen at Ticonderoga. In addition to supplying some 1500 men to the Continental Army, the area was a vital source of rations and funds for that Army.

Fifteen families comprised the first group of settlers. John Minor, only 30 years old but already head of a family of six children, was the leader.

The Fundamental Act, an arrangement for dividing the land in the new settlement, was signed by Minor and four others. Under the Act, bachelors got only ten acres but could have two more when they took a wife. The maximum for any one family was set at 75 acres. The original plots were free and awarded by drawing lots.

It was in Woodbury that the Reverend Samuel Seabury of Groton was elected the first Protestant Episcopal Bishop in America, and both Generals U.S. Grant and William T. Sherman are descended from Woodbury people.

Today the little town is a flourishing dairy center, and boasts five churches. The first Meeting House was built in the 1680's.

The Village Green. One of the town's five churches crowns the village green.

188

St. Paul's Church. The Episcopal Church, built close to the road, was erected in 1785, but has been altered since. (Open)

The Rectory. After the church was built, the low house was joined to the edifice by a covered passageway. It was the rectory of the Reverend John M. Marshall, a priest of the Church of England. Part of the house may have been built as early as 1700.

Bacon House. A wealthy merchant named Jabez Bacon lived in the house, built in about 1762. He is said to have amassed a fortune of a half million dollars during the Revolution. Daniel Curtis, a leading mill owner, also owned the house.

Curtis Store. In the early 1800's, Daniel Curtis made German silver trinkets in this house which were then sold by peddlers. In its early days, it was a neighborhood meeting place and was later used by a tinsmith.

The Glebe. Started in 1690 by the Reverend Nathan Hurd, this weathered saltbox later became the residence of the Reverend Mr. Marshall, who was a Tory. It was in this house that Samuel Seabury was elected Bishop in 1783. Eventually the house was sold to raise money for the Parish. Now a museum, it contains original furniture and early documents. (Open)

The Glebe. In the paneled fireplace wall is a closet with a split door. It was in this room that the dignitaries of the church met when they elected Bishop Seabury.

191

The Glebe. In the closet is a small hinged door that opens into a secret stairway to the basement. It is said to have been constructed to enable the Tory priest to escape to the hills if ever the loyalists came to seize him.

The Glebe. Among the furnishings from the early days are the kitchen table and chairs and the spinningwheel.

The Glebe. A handsome chest-on-chest
and antique chairs grace the parlor of
the old house.

Curtis House. Built in 1754 and
greaty enlarged since stagecoach days,
the building is still operated as a hotel.

193

MORRISTOWN

NEW JERSEY

At the time of the Revolution, Morristown, which owed its early development to rich deposits of iron ore, was one of the most important sources of iron in the colonies. Some 45 forges operated in the town and vicinity during the war and provided cannons and shot for the Continental Army. In addition, Colonel Jacob Ford and his son, also a colonel, set up a powder mill there.

The town on the banks of the Whippany River was settled about 1710 and at first was known as New Hanover. It was renamed Morristown in 1740, after Governor Lewis Morris.

Neither the British nor the Hessians were able to occupy Morristown during the war, because General Washington kept soldiers there in recognition of its importance as a supply base. He led his army there first in 1777 for their winter encampment, and again in 1779–80. The men were quartered in rude huts in an area called Jockey Hollow.

The British did launch one attack against Morristown in 1780 but a thunderstorm broke it up. Frontier troops of the Continental Army, encouraged by handbills distributed by the British and activities of British agents, staged a mutiny at Morristown in 1781, but it was called off ten days later.

Morristown National Historical Park, established through the efforts of local citizens to preserve important traditions, includes many remaining or reconstructed landmarks in the area utilized during the Revolution.

Ford House. Colonel Jacob Ford, Jr., a Revolutionary powdermaker and iron manufacturer, built this fine house in 1774. He offered it to General Washington and his family in 1779–80 as a temporary home and headquarters while the Continental Army was encamped nearby, and Morristown became the military capital of the colonies. It has a wide hall and splendid old furnishings used by Washington, Lafayette, and other Revolutionary generals. The house now is a museum. (Open)

Ford House. This graceful secretary with ball feet and arched panel doors is one of several fine antiques in the drawing room.

Ford House. Rope springs support the mattress of the simple bed in a second floor bedroom.

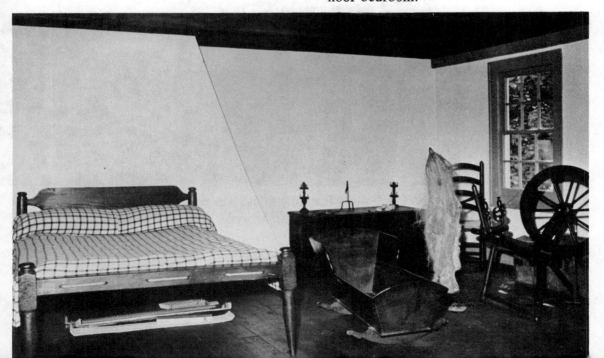

Dr. Jabez Campbell House. In 1779, this well-shaded house was the scene of Alexander Hamilton's successful courtship of Elizabeth Schuyler. It was erected in 1760.

Mills House. The little house was built in about 1740 by Captain Lincoln Mills. The interior, more impressive than the outside, has heavy molded mantels and paneled overmantels.

Wick House. Built in about 1746 near Jockey Hollow, the little farmhouse was the residence of Captain Henry Wick of the colonial cavalry and was later the headquarters of Major General Arthur St. Clair, a scotsman, during the encampment of the Continental Army. It is furnished as a farmhouse of the period. (Open)

Wick House. The old kitchen cabinet stands in front of a plank wall.

Wick House. Among the relics to be enjoyed are this unusual two-place wagon seat and a candle stand.

Army Hospital. This is a reproduction of an army hospital used by the Continental Army during its encampment in the area.

Alfred Vail House. In this frame building, erected in the early 1800's, Samuel F.B. Morse and Arthur Vail developed the magnetic telegraph in 1837. Three miles of wire were stretched about the building, and the first message transmitted on the telegraph instrument was "A patient waiter is no loser."

PRINCETON

NEW JERSEY

The history of this beautiful town really starts when Princeton University was moved there from Newark in 1756. However, it had been settled in 1696 by six Quaker families, who were preceded in 1681 by Captain Henry Greenland, whose plantation occupied most of the site of the town.

At first, it was known as Stony Brook, then as Prince's Town, which was later shortened. Until the University came, it was best known as a coaching center on the main highway half way between New York and Philadelphia.

During the Revolution, when its residents were known to be staunch advocates of independence, the town became an object of Tory bitterness. As a result, Princeton's farms were plundered and her crops destroyed by the British.

In an all-night march after the Battle of Trenton, General Washington led his victorious troops to Princeton, where they won another encounter by routing two regiments of British. Washington then led them out of the path of Cornwallis' pursuing army to their winter encampment at Morristown.

From June to November in 1783, Princeton was the nation's temporary capital, when the Continental Congress fled Philadelphia in the face of threats of violence by unpaid soldiers.

Washington lived in the area for three months at that time and while there wrote his Farewell Address to the Continental Army.

Berrien House (Rockingham). The clapboarded fieldstone house with a double balcony across the back was erected in 1730. General Washington resided there in 1783 while Congress met at Princeton to draft peace terms with England. It was here that he wrote his Farewell Address. A tenement until a few years ago, the house is now a museum with furniture and objects used by Washington. (Open)

Quaker Meeting House. Until 1757, this was the only place of worship in Princeton, having been built in 1726. Buried there are Richard Stockton, a signer of the Declaration of Independence, and Governor Charles S. Olden.

Thomas Clark Farmhouse. General Mercer of the Continental Army was carried here after the Battle of Princeton and died of his wounds. His bloodstains still can be seen on the floor of the pre-Revolutionary building.

Beatty House. This was the pre-Revolutionary home of Colonel Erkuries Beatty of the Continental Army, an aide to Lafayette. It later served as a girls' school.

Nassau Hall. This lantern adorns the top of Nassau Hall, the first building erected on the campus of Princeton University. The ivy-covered, sandstone structure was erected in 1756 by Robert Smith. It was here that the Continental Congress, frightened out of Philadelphia, received the news of the peace treaty ending the Revolutionary War. (Open)

Revolutionary Cannon. In the main quadrangle back of Nassau Hall, this old cannon used in the Battle of Princeton is buried to the breach to prevent its removal by exuberant students.

Battle Monument. In a small park at a main intersection in the middle of town is this 50-foot block of limestone, showing in relief the figure of General Washington leading his troops. It was designed by Frederick W. MacMonnies.

203

Morven. The long yellow brick house, with balancing wings, was started in 1701 by Richard Stockton, a signer of the Declaration of Independence. Cornwallis made his headquarters there in 1776. Washington, Lafayette, and Rochambeau were among many prominent men entertained there.

Morven. Beautiful portraits and paintings adorn the walls of the dining room and other rooms in the mansion.

Morven. The drawing room contains a severely carved mantel and fine old furniture.

Morven. A double archway separates two charming parlors.

Alexander Hall. The large brick building erected in 1813 is the first structure built to serve as a seminary in America by the Presbyterian Church.

Thomas Olden House. From this modest house, built in 1696, General Washington reviewed his troops. He also used it as a hospital. Once the home of a trapper, it now stands on the grounds of a large estate.

BORDENTOWN

NEW JERSEY

Prominent persons from Philadelphia, including the Morrises, Chews, and Hopkinsons, enjoyed Bordentown as a gracious summer resort in pre-Revolutionary days. Situated on a bluff overlooking the Delaware River south of Trenton, the town was settled in 1682 by Thomas Farnsworth, an English Quaker, and at first was known as Farnsworth's Landing.

As early as 1734, it was a busy shipping center and had stage and packet service to Philadelphia and Perth Amboy. The service was established by Colonel Joseph Borden, after whom the town was renamed.

In the Revolution, the British burned the home and store of Colonel Borden because patriots had built powder kegs in his cooperage, with which they intended to destroy the British fleet that was anchored at Philadelphia. The kegs did little damage, however, since the fleet had been moved. The Redcoats took their revenge anyhow.

Thomas Paine, the fiery political author and philosopher, lived in Bordentown in 1783 and later. He was visited there by Benjamin Franklin and other prominent men.

John Fitch, the inventor, sailed his first commercially operated steam packet to Bordentown in 1790, and again two years later.

In 1816, Joseph Bonaparte, brother of Napoleon and exiled King of Spain, established a large estate there.

Joseph Hopkinson House. Now a military school dormitory, the house once was owned by Joseph Hopkinson, son of Francis Hopkinson, and the author of "Hail Columbia." It was built about 1740.

Hoagland's Tavern. Originally owned by Colonel Oakley Hoagland, the tavern was sacked by Hessian troops before the Battle of Trenton in 1776.

Borden House. This is the rebuilt pre-Revolutionary home of Colonel Borden. It was burned by the British in 1778 as a retaliatory measure.

Francis Hopkinson House. A date of 1750 appears on the gable of this house, built by Joseph Imlay, a merchant. An early owner, Francis Hopkinson, was a signer of the Declaration of Independence, representative to the Continental Congress, and Chairman of the Naval Board in the first two years of the Revolution. Some believe he was the designer of the Stars and Stripes.

Patience Wright House. This is the pre-Revolutionary home of the first American sculptress and mother of Joseph Wright, the American portrait artist who designed the Great Seal of the State of New Jersey.

Thomas Paine House. The late 18th century house was the home of Thomas Paine, the so-called Revolutionary firebrand, during one of his stays in Bordentown.

Hilton House. Part of the house, built in 1750, was made of bricks said to have been brought from England. Its owner, William Hilton, conducted a private school there.

SALEM

NEW JERSEY

Situated a few miles back from the Delaware River below Camden, Salem was settled in 1675 by English Quakers under the leadership of John Fenwick. There had been brief visits earlier by Dutch and Swedes, but those would-be settlers moved inland, after a brief stay.

The town was declared a Port of Entry in 1682 by Royal Commission, but after the British bottled up the port during the Revolution, Salem lost its shipping trade to Philadelphia which had superior facilities.

In 1778, General Washington sent men commanded by Anthony Wayne from Valley Forge to obtain supplies.

Beef from the Salem area helped to save the Continental troops after the British sent a detachment from Philadelphia in a vain attempt to foil the mission.

The British went there later to forage led by Colonel Mawhood, but wound up massacring all but a few men out of a colonial detachment of 90 sleeping soldiers. Earlier, colonial militia had compelled the British to retreat to Salem from nearby Quinton Bridge, after an American detachment had been ambushed there. A monument at the site of the bridge commemorates the action.

Otherwise, life in the early days of Salem was fairly peaceful.

Joseph Darkin House. Known for its handsome brick work, the sturdy farmhouse with the steep roof was built in 1720, according to a date on the gable end.

Isaac Smart House. Built in 1696, this country home is made of brick which had been covered with plaster. It is believed that the handsome interior woodwork was styled by ships' carpenters.

Isaac Smart House. The small parlor fireplace has an interestingly carved overmantel under the exposed ceiling beams.

Isaac Smart House. The massive grandfather clock stands at the foot of the stairway.

Holmeland. The three-part brick house was started in 1729 and enlarged in 1784. It was the home of Colonel Holme, who owned 1600 acres and a ferry. The British set fire to the house in 1778. It is furnished with early American pieces.

Guilford Hall. R. G. Johnson, historian, built the house in about 1687. It is said to be Salem's oldest building.

John Jones' Law Office. This small octagonal structure, built in about 1732, is reported to have been the first brick law office in the thirteen colonies. It stands back of the Salem County Office Building, built in 1806.

Alexander Grant House. Built in 1721, the house is now a museum of the Salem County Historical Society. It contains many fine exhibits, including period furniture, rare china, and Wistarburg glass. (Open)

Salem Oak. Said to be more than 500 years old, this huge tree located in the Friends' Burying Ground is more than 80 feet tall.

Hancock House. This is the locale of the massacre of 1778, It was built in 1734 by William and Sarah Hancock and is now a State museum. The building date is shown in the brickwork on the end of the house. (Open)

Hancock House. An unusual book closet with a paneled door is built-in next to the fireplace in a second-floor bedroom.

Hancock House. On the attic floor under the relics are traces of the blood-stains resulting from the massacre.

Alloway's Creek Meeting House. Still in its original interior condition, the Meeting House was erected in 1756 and remained in regular use until recently. (Open)

Alloways' Creek Meeting House. A sturdy paneled wall separated the sexes in the otherwise austere interior of the Meeting House.

Grist Mill. In about 1740 Robert Simpson built the large stone mill which provided grain for Washington's army.

WASHINGTON CROSSING

PENNSYLVANIA

Technically, Washington Crossing was not a town at the time of the stirring event which took place there. Perhaps it wasn't even a hamlet, but nevertheless it is an historic place with a ferry house, farm house, and other old buildings nearby. It is where on Christmas Night in 1776 General Washington led his ragged troops across the Delaware River in flat boats. The troops then marched all night, and in the morning fought and won the Battle of Trenton, a crucial turning point in this country's fight for freedom.

To commemorate these events, Washington Crossing State Park has been established by the State of Pennsylvania. Various monuments and memorials have been added to the historic buildings which stand nearby, including fine old houses that once served as headquarters for officers of the Continental Army.

Point of Embarkation. A monument marks the approximate point from where General Washington's 2400 troops started their memorable crossing of the Delaware River.

219

Thompson-Neely House. The house, built in about 1702 by John Pidcock, the first white settler in the area, was at the time of the crossing the headquarters of General Lord Stirling and Lieutenant James Monroe, later to become the fifth President of the United States. It is here that General Washington is believed to have conferred with his officers to perfect plans for the crossing, although the location of the conference is disputed by some. At the time of the Revolution, the house was one room deep and two stories high.

Thompson-Neely House. This is the room where the crossing is said to have been planned by Washington and his staff.

Thompson-Neely House. An over-size bed warmer leans against the plain fireplace in the parlor.

Thompson-Neely House. Fine china is seen in a corner cupboard.

Thompson-Neely House. With its high-chair, low chair, and cradle, this room is equipped for children.

Dr. Chapman House. This pre-Revolutionary home was, during the Delaware Crossing Campaign, the headquarters of Colonel Henry Knox, a close friend and advisor of General Washington, and Captain Alexander Hamilton, later to become Secretary of the Treasury.

Merrick House. Built in 1731, this was the headquarters of General Nathanael Greene and is believed by some to be the real place from where the Crossing was planned.

Hayhurst. General John Sullivan used Hayhurst, another pre-Revolutionary house, as his headquarters. It has two adjacent front doors of different heights, indicating it may once have been two houses.

NEW CASTLE

DELAWARE

William Penn first landed on American soil at New Castle in 1682 after James, Duke of York, had conveyed to him all land within a radius of 12 miles of the town.

However, New Castle had been founded earlier in 1651 by the Dutch under Peter Stuyvesant, on the site of a former Indian village. It was the first town to be laid out in Delaware, the meeting place of all colonial assemblies, and the first state capital.

The original name was Fort Casimir, later changed to Trafaldigheets, or Trinity, following its capture by the Swedes in 1654. Then, after the Dutch recaptured the town and ownership was changed from the West India Company to The Burgomasters of Amsterdam in 1656, it was known as New Amstel. It kept that name until the British, under the leadership of Sir Robert Carr, routed the Dutch in 1664 and changed the name to New Castle. By 1657, there were 100 buildings in the town.

The Dutch seized the town again in 1673, but it was returned to Great Britain the following year.

Lord Baltimore contested the grant to Penn, and the boundary disputes were not settled until after a survey conducted in 1763–67 by Charles Mason and Jeremiah Dixon, establishing what is now known as the Mason and Dixon Line. The spire atop the Courthouse in New Castle was used as the central point of the 12-mile arc which forms the northern boundary of Delaware and part of the Mason and Dixon Line.

Two signers of the Declaration of Independence—George Read and Thomas McKean—were from New Castle. Read and Gunning Bedford signed the Constitution.

The Academy. The large building, which adjoins the church, was started about 1798. After serving as a private and semi-private school, it became a public school and is now leased to the church. It is believed to have been built by Peter Crowding, who erected many early buildings in New Castle.

Immanuel Church. The altar was originally at the opposite end of the church.

Immanuel Church. The brick edifice, covered with stucco, was started about 1703; the tower and spire were added later. The church silver includes a flagon which was donated by the Governor of Pennsylvania in 1710. Many local notables are buried in the churchyard, including George Read. (Open)

225

Read House. This house, the most imposing in New Castle, was built in about 1801 by George Read, son of the signer. A long hall running from the entrance to the garden door at the rear is broken by two archways. The first floor has a 13-foot high ceiling and wide swinging mahogany doors.

Van Leuvenigh House. Named after Zachariah van Leuvenigh, a chief magistrate of New Castle who bought it in 1765, the house is thought to have been built around 1760. Among its interior features are interesting woodwork and a fireplace of unusual design.

Gunning Bedford House. John van Gezel, a grandson of one of the original founders of New Castle, built the house in about 1730. It later became the home of Governor Gunning Bedford and still later was purchased by another governor, Caleb Bennett, who used it as a hotel. The stoop was added when the grading of the street was changed.

The Courthouse. This was the original capitol of the State. The central part was built in 1732, and wings were added in 1765, but have been revised since then. It was converted to commercial use after the capital was moved to Dover in 1777 but has been restored as a museum with State funds. (Open)

The Courthouse. The courtroom occupied the first floor of the central portion of the old building.

The Village Green. The large green runs back from the courthouse, with early homes on one side and old buildings on the other.

Old Dutch House. This is the garden view of the house, now a furnished museum, which stands flush with the sidewalk and down one step in front. It was built in the 1600's and stands in its original form. (Open)

Old Dutch House. The kitchen fireplace is unusually high and narrow.

Old Dutch House. A flannel nightshirt and high-waisted pantaloons hang on the door of a bedroom closet.

Old Dutch House. Even this simple house has a chair rail in its well-furnished dining room.

Kensey Johns, Sr., House. The kitchen wing is believed to have been built about 1685 as the home of Ambrose Baker, a wealthy Dutchman. The front was constructed in 1789–90 by Kensey Johns, who was a chief justice of Delaware's Supreme Court. The house has interesting wall paneling and marble-faced fireplaces surmounted by delicate carved woodwork.

Senator Nicholas Van Dyke House. This symmetrical house was built in 1799 by the Senator. It has splendid interior decoration.

DOVER

DELAWARE

The site of this town was part of an estate of 800 acres belonging to John and Richard Walker, who had bought the Indian rights in 1680 for "three match-coats, 12 bottles of drink, and four handfuls of powder."

Although William Penn gave orders in 1683 to erect a county seat at Dover, nothing was done about laying out the town until 1717, when the Delaware Assembly appointed commissioners for that purpose. The once quiet town they laid out is in an agricultural area near the center of the tiny state.

An early courthouse on the site of the present one is said to have been ordered burned in order to salvage the nails.

For many years, Dover was an important stagecoach stop on the King's Road leading from Philadelphia down to Lewes.

In the town are two old churches, built in 1734 and 1790. The first, Christ Church, remains in regular use, while the other, the Old Presbyterian Church, is now a state museum, open to the public.

The town became the capital of the state in 1777, and on December 7, 1787, a convention of 30 delegates meeting there unanimously ratified the United States Constitution, giving Delaware the honor of being the first state of the new union.

Fears for the safety of the Capital were expressed when the British fleet cruised into Delaware Bay during the War of 1812, but nothing of importance occurred.

Aspendale. Charles Numbers erected this plantation house in 1771, and ever since it has been in the possession of his descendants. It still has all of its original woodwork and paneling and the original coat of paint. The original lead roof was melted down for bullets during the Revolution.

The Paton House. The central section was built prior to 1780 by the Reverend John Miller, pastor of the Dover Presbyterian Church and father of Professor Samuel Miller, a Revolutionary captain and the founder of Princeton Theological Seminary. Later the house was the residence of the Saulsbury family, including Senator Eli Saulsbury and Gove Saulsbury, Governor of Delaware.

Old State House. Located at the end of the village green laid out in 1717, this building where Delaware ratified the Federal Constitution was built in 1722. It has been rebuilt and restored several times. It is the second oldest state house in the United States that is still in use. It has fine early portraits of George Washington and early Delaware patriots. (Open)

Old State House. The delicate ceiling light is surrounded by excellent decoration.

Old State House. The beautiful stairway leads to the second floor.

Sykes House. James Sykes, a noted surgeon, built this brick house with the eyebrow windows on its top floor in 1812. Many eminent lawyers have resided there.

Bradford-Loockerman House. Vincent Loockerman, a merchant and land owner, built the house in 1742. It is known for its interior woodwork, Philadelphia furniture, and early portraits.

The Old Academy. A treasurer of Delaware, John Banning, who erected the house in 1706, reimbursed Revolutionary soldiers with hard cash to replace depreciated currency they had received. A basement room contains magnificent hand-hewn oak beams.

Dickinson Mansion. Now a State museum, the mansion was erected in 1740 by Judge Samuel Dickinson, whose son, John, became a governor of Delaware. It is furnished with 18th century antiques, some of which John Dickinson owned when he resided there. (Open)

Dickinson Mansion. The tea table and other early furniture are placed in the parlor.

Dickinson Mansion. This is one end of the parlor.

LEWES
DELAWARE

Since it was first settled by the Dutch in 1631, Lewes, located at the mouth of the Delaware River, has had more than its share of names. The Indians called it Sikeoness; the Dutch referred to it as Zwaanendael and Hoorn; it then came to be called Fort Opdike and Whorekill; the British knew it as Deale, and it later came to be called Lewistown and Lewestown. Finally, in about 1682 after the arrival of the English under William Penn, the name was changed to Lewes, after a town of that name in Sussex County, England.

After the first settlement was wiped out by the Indians, a second settlement was made in 1658–59 with a trading post and fort and was reinforced in 1663 by a group of 41 Mennonites under Peter Cornelis Plockhoy. This colony was destroyed by the British under Sir Robert Carr, and the town was transferred to British sovereignty in 1664.

Lewes is best known as the home of Delaware River pilots, as an early shipbuilding and fishing center, and as the place where a jury of 12 women was empaneled for a murder trial in 1683. The good women cleared a husband suspected of having murdered his wife. It was also the birthplace of three governors of Delaware and the home of three others.

Pirates raided Lewes in 1690 and again in 1698, and the notorious Captain Kidd made Lewes a port of call in 1700 while on a voyage from the West Indies.

A British man-of-war seized some prisoners in a raid during the winter of 1779–80 but released them on payment of 100 bullocks. In the War of 1812, there was a two-day bombardment of Lewes, but little damage was done.

Cannon Ball (David Rowland) House. This neglected downtown house, awaiting renovation and preservation by the Lewes Historical Society, is one of the few in the country struck by enemy gunfire in the War of 1812, when the British frigates *Poitiers* and *Belvidere* blockaded the mouth of the Delaware River. A cannonball is said to have struck the foundation in the lower left end of the front of the house. It was built prior to 1797. The otherwise undistinguished house contains three mantels.

238

Maull House. When restored, the early Dutch-type house is to be the headquarters of the local D.A.R. Chapter. It was built in about 1750 and may be the house where Jerome Bonaparte and his bride, Elizabeth Patterson, found shelter after being shipwrecked in the storm of 1803.

Maull House. Opening of this fireplace revealed the unusual herringbone pattern in the brickwork at the back.

Fisher House. Colonel Henry Fisher, a Revolutionary patriot and pilot, built the house between 1780 and 1790. It was later the home of Colonel Samuel Boyer, who commanded the town's defenses in the War of 1812.

Fisher House. Wainscoting and other paneling are seen in the entrance hall.

Fisher House. Fine decoration remains in the cornice and fireplace in the parlor, together with wood paneling.

Methodist Meeting House. The first Methodist Meeting in Lewes was held in this house in 1791.

Hall House. This was the home of Colonel David Hall, a governor of Delaware. Built about 1790, it has one of the most handsome interiors of all Lewes houses.

Hall House. Original plaster ornamentation is seen in the cornice in the entrance hall.

Hitchens House. George Whitefield, the English evangelist, preached in this house, and it is believed that Francis Asbury preached there also. It was built around 1740.

ELKTON
MARYLAND

The British are said to have carried off the early records of Elkton. The town was first known as Head of Elk because of its location on the Elk River, which flows into Chesapeake Bay at its head.

At least one house, the Hermitage, remains of those built as early as 1735. In 1772, Elkton produced pottery, but in its early days it was known chiefly as a shipping port and a source of food for Baltimore, which lies on the Bay some 50 miles away. It became the seat of Cecil County in 1786.

The rest of Elkton's history is bound up with coincidental events during the Revolution. Jacob Hollingsworth had a hostelry there in which he entertained both George Washington and his adversary, Lord Howe, within the space of 24 hours. He used the same bed for both.

Then, too, Robert Alexander, owner of the Hermitage and a well-known Tory, entertained both Washington and Lafayette and also Lord Howe. On one occasion in 1777, he had a sumptuous repast ready for British officers until Lafayette and his troops galloped up and ate the meal.

Washington had heard that the British under Lord Howe were sailing up Chesapeake Bay and Washington hastened to Elkton attempting to assure that no supplies would be available there to the enemy. He dined with Alexander and when he learned that his host was a Royalist, Washington realized his mission would be a failure. The next day the British arrived, ate Alexander's food, and burnt his fences for firewood. Fearing that he would be hanged by the local court, Alexander and his family fled to London.

Elkton became notorious in more recent years as a sort of Gretna Green, where quick marriages could be arranged, but that activity was eventually deflated.

Graymount. The older part of the house, situated on the summit of Gray's Hill, was built in 1769. It was from this vantage point that General Washington is said to have watched Lord Howe's army disembark for their march on Philadelphia. The splendid view the site afforded in all directions has all but disappeared, as surrounding trees have grown tall. The author's father was born in this house in 1874.

Graymount. Paneling surrounds the drawing room windows in the foot-thick walls, with window seats below.

The Hermitage. After Robert Alexander, the Tory, entertained British officers here in 1777, local patriots confiscated his estate, and it was divided up. The spacious house was built in 1735.

Mitchell House. Dr. Abraham Mitchell, physician and scholar, built the house in 1769. It was used as a hospital during the Revolution and now is a public library. (Open)

Mitchell House. The front parlor is distinguished by elaborate plaster ornamentation.

Partridge Hall. The Veterans of Foreign Wars now occupy the building erected in 1768. It has interior cornices, mantels, and interesting paneling.

Hollingsworth Tavern. When Washington and Lord Howe spent consecutive nights here, they are said not only to have used the same bed but to have had the attentions of the same servant. The old tavern built in about 1750 is now used for business offices.

247

Gilpin Manor. The large farmhouse on the outskirts of town was built in 1760 by Joseph Gilpin. It has spacious rooms with huge double doors.

CHESTERTOWN

MARYLAND

A charming old town on the Chester River near the north end of Maryland's famed Eastern Shore, Chestertown had a "tea party" on the same day that Boston had its own famous party, and for the same reason. The ship whose cargo was jettisoned was the Brigantine *Geddes*.

Chestertown also has other distinctions. For one thing, it has been the home of four United States Senators: Philip Reed, Ezekial Freeman Chambers, James Alfred Pearce, and Robert Wright. It was also the home of George Vickers, who was the senior naval officer in the U.S. Navy at the time of his death and had been commander of the U.S.S. Constellation, one of the country's earliest men-of-war.

A more dubious distinction came from Bishop Francis Asbury, who called Chestertown a wicked place, following a visit there after the Revolution. The town was said to have been "a center of colorful fashion and frivolity, peopled by dandies who wore unpowdered wigs and embroidered waistcoats." Horse racing was started there in 1750. Schools were closed and courts were adjourned during the annual races. It is written that gentlemen from Virginia wagered their slaves on the outcome of those races.

There were reports, too, that Chestertown had a spendthrift reputation and that smuggling and gambling were rife. One observer said: "Foppery, idleness, and dissipation are striding briskly along to bring about a change in the perspective for our land. The incoming cargoes of trash this year are astonishing."

Chestertown was one of the earliest settlements on the Eastern Shore, having been founded in 1706 by the Provincial Assembly on land owned by Samuel Wilmer. It was an active shipping center in its early days and had a ropewalk and ships' chandlers. Its ships traded with England, the West Indies, Spain, and Africa.

To its cultural credit, Chestertown is the seat of Washington College, established in 1782 and named with his consent after George Washington, who became a member of its Board of Visitors and Governors and contributed $233.33 to the institution.

The old town, still on the small side, was surrounded by splendid plantation homes, many of which still stand today.

Rock of Ages (Palmer) House. This simple stone house probably was built before 1700, perhaps in 1692, and is the town's oldest. It has walls two feet thick, hand-carved mantels, random flooring, and paneled window frames.

White Swan Tavern. Once a popular and thriving hostelry, built about 1750, the brick structure is now a store building.

Historical Society House. Known as the Wescott House, the three-and-a-half story home erected in about 1730 is now the headquarters of the Historical Society of Kent County. (Open)

250

Historical Society House. Built-in cabinets and bookcases flank the fireplace in
the parlor, which has a chair rail and a
paneled opening to the front of the house.

Wickes House. This pre-Revolutionary
building was once a tavern operated by
Samuel Beck. Despite its age, it is one of
the finer houses in Chestertown.

Wickes House. This large and delight-
ful garden is screened by a brick wall.

Widehall. This is the front entrance
to one of Chestertown's largest and finest
houses, built about 1762 on the bank of
the Chester River. Two U.S. Senators—
Robert Wright and Ezekial Chambers—
once lived there.

Custom House. Although it was built prior to 1710 when Chestertown's overseas trade began to swell, it is said that the old Custom House was never used as such, becoming a residence instead.

The Bank of the Chester River. The river from which the town takes its name is lined with old houses, some built before the Revolution, but their entrances are all on the street side. The Custom House is the last building on the left.

EASTON
MARYLAND

Here is the social, political, economic, and geographical center of Maryland's famed Eastern Shore. Once named Talbot Courthouse, and later Talbot Town, Easton was incorporated in 1785, though in 1710 the Court at the then nearby town of York spent 115,000 pounds of tobacco for a new brick building to house the Court there and paid 5,000 pounds of tobacco for two acres of land. However, the present courthouse was not built until 1794, on land surveyed by John Needles.

The construction of the courthouse had been preceded by the building of a Friends' Meeting House in 1682–83.

A commission composed of Jeremiah and Greenbury Goldsborough and three other citizens appointed by the State Assembly was charged with buying the land for the courthouse and laying it out. The Goldsboroughs were members of a prominent local family.

Easton is located at the head of the Tred Avon River and, like Chestertown, is surrounded by colonial mansions, which make it an historical showplace in "the land of pleasant living."

Residents of the town were prominent in opposing the Stamp Tax and other oppressive measures in pre-Revolutionary days.

Hughlett Henry House. This deep and narrow downtown house, erected in about 1795, is now commercially occupied. (Open)

Old Frame Hotel. Built in the early 1800's, the stark old wooden building, which once served as a hotel, has a brick fireplace in the basement and a spiral stairway with curved balusters between the second and third floors. The small upstairs rooms were hotel bedrooms. It now houses a hardware store. (Open)

The Brick Hotel. Across from the Old Frame Hotel is a brick hotel, built in 1812, which for a time was the leading hostelry on the Eastern Shore and a prominent meeting place for important people of the day. It is now an office building. (Open)

Talbot County Courthouse. The first courthouse on this site was built in 1710 but the handsome existing structure was erected in 1794 and enlarged in 1958. (Open)

Talbot County Courthouse. This is the spacious courtroom on the second floor of the courthouse.

Third Haven Meeting House. The modest frame building is believed to be the oldest frame structure dedicated to religious use that still exists in the country. It was built in 1682. William Penn is said to have preached there, with Lord Baltimore present, soon after it was opened. It was a source of considerable controversy in 1781 when some members insisted that religious zeal should give sufficient warmth to make a stove unnecessary. Some people came by boat in the early days to attend services. The Meeting House acquired its saltbox look when it was enlarged later on. (Open)

Historical Society House. A fine example of Federal architecture, the four-story town house was built in the late 1790's. It has herringbone carving and a brick-floored kitchen. (Open)

Tilghman's Fortune. Hidden in a grove of trees behind a commercial establishment which occupies what was once its front yard, the house was built before 1800 by a Captain Vickers on land patented to Admiral Samuel Tilghman in 1659.

Ratcliffe Manor. Ivy covers most of the front of the imposing house built in 1749 by Richard Hollyday on a tract of land facing the Tred Avon River. The tract was patented by Captain Robert Morris in 1659. It has a fine box garden.

Ratcliffe Manor. The fireplace end of the drawing room is paneled to the ceiling with hardwood.

Ratcliffe Manor. There is a window seat below each paneled window recess in the dining room.

Old Bloomfield. The long white brick house with its five dormers and two front entrances was erected on the Tred Avon River about 1690. It was built by either Thomas or John Bartlett. In the parlor is a fireplace with an elliptical hood.

Old Bloomfield. An unusual four overhang is seen above a wall in the of the house. It may have been a when the dormers were construct

ST. MICHAELS

MARYLAND

The British can take full credit for the prominence that St. Michaels enjoys today, for their attack on the little town on the Miles River in 1813 assured its place in the history of the area.

The story goes that one Captain Dodson was commander of a local battery located in the woods on Parritt's Point near St. Michaels, when the British tried to surprise the town from the river under cover of fog and drizzle. The American troops fled, all but Dodson and two men, who fired at point blank range a cannon loaded with scrap iron that killed 27 of the British invaders. The rest of the British troops, it is said, fled the scene, leaving among the dead a nephew of British Admiral Cockburn.

However, the British officially told a different story, saying that they drove into the town, spiked the American guns, destroyed stores and ammunition, and re-embarked with a loss of only two men wounded.

It is also said that, to thwart a threatened British attack from the river, Brigadier Perry Benson ordered all lights in the town put out, except lanterns hung high in trees, so the enemy would fire over the roofs of the town.

Settled in the early 1700's St. Michaels for a time was a thriving riverport and ship-building center, boasting at one time of 25 boatyards, which turned out punts, schooners, skipjacks, log canoes, and larger craft. One of the latter, the sailing brig *John Gilpin,* held the trans-Pacific record from Peru to China for seven years. The ship-building peak was from 1810 to around 1830, although by 1820 many yards had been abandoned. Today it is a center for oystering and crabbing.

In its earlier days, St. Michaels, located west of Easton, was described as a place "where the aristocratic planter and the waterman fused."

The Inn. The old brick inn, once a thriving hostelry, but unoccupied when this photograph was made, stands on the main street and was built in 1817 by Wrightson Jones, who operated a shipyard nearby.

St. Mary's Square. This quaint village green in the center of town was laid out in the 1770's by James Braddock, an Englishman. In addition to the cannon, it contains the town bell, seen standing high on a pole just to the right of the center of the photograph.

Amelia Welby House. This was the birthplace of the local poetess whose work was praised by Edgar Allen Poe. It was built prior to 1819.

Cannon Ball House. A cannon ball, fired by the British from a ship on the Miles River in the bombardment of 1813, is said to have dropped through the roof of this house, built before 1800. It stands near St. Mary's Square.

Log Houses. This dwelling is composed of two small log houses which have been joined and covered with clapboards. It dates from before the Revolution. The land was patented by John Hollingsworth in 1659.

Crooked Intention. Just outside town stands this rambling brick house, the first part of which was built in about 1717 and added to in about 1730 by Robert Harrison on a grant of 130 acres to Hugh Sherwood by Lord Baltimore in 1681. Six dormers and four chimneys grace the roofline of this charming old dwelling.

Crooked Intention. Near the home are the original meat house and dairy.

San Domingo. Joseph Harrison built the house in about 1803 on land patented in 1695. Early dependencies and a Harrison graveyard are located near the house. It has a winding staircase and the original floors of pine and walnut remain, along with old beams in the kitchen.

Mt. Misery. The house probably was built about 1805 by Edward Cooey, a slave dealer, on a tract of 100 acres patented in 1667 to Thomas Hethod. The old house was dilapidated in the mid-1950's but has been restored.

Mt. Misery. This stairway is so narrow that a hole had to be cut in the ceiling to admit furniture to the second floor.

OXFORD
MARYLAND

Here is one of Maryland's oldest towns. Oxford was settled in 1635, and was declared a Port of Entry in 1669. At that time, it was one of the state's two leading settlements, the other being Annapolis.

For a brief time it was known both as Williamstadt and as Thread Haven. The name of its river, the Tred Avon, is a corruption of the former name. It may have gotten its present name from Oxford University in England.

It soon became an active port, exporting tobacco, pork, wheat, and lumber, and importing slaves and also rope, thread, hemp, cordage, and various ships' supplies. Two hundred vessels were registered in the Custom House at the same time in the mid 1700's.

Oystering, crabbing, and ship-building were its principal activities, aside from its overseas trade. That trade was handled by representatives of merchants in London and Liverpool, who maintained factories or warehouses in Oxford under the supervision of local factors. One of the latter was Robert Morris, son of a sailor and father of the financier of the American Revolution, who later became a shipping merchant in his own name. He was killed by a shot fired from a vessel during a celebration held in his honor.

The town originally was laid out in 1684 by a philanthropist named Margaret Lowe and received its charter on order of Lord Baltimore in 1695.

The last trans-Atlantic vessel called there in 1775, its trade having gradually been lost to Baltimore. Still today, Oxford retains its boatyards, which turn out small craft for the pleasure and fishing trade.

Comesbury. An extensive, well-kept lawn leads from the front of the house to Island Creek. The large house was built about 1740.

Plimhimmon. This was the residence of the widow of Colonel Tench Tilghman. It was erected in about 1736 on a grant to Edward Lloyd. Tilghman, a Revolutionary hero who lived elsewhere in Talbot County, was selected by his friend George Washington to carry the message announcing Cornwallis' surrender at Yorktown to the Continental Congress meeting in Philadelphia.

Tilghman Monument. Now a part of Oxford Cemetery, the old Tilghman family graveyard contains a monument to Colonel Tilghman, erected by his wife, who is buried there. Tilghman's body, however, is buried at Baltimore.

Barnaby House. This simple clap-boarded house, standing next to the side-walk, apparently was built in the early 1700's. It contains pine woodwork and an interesting hand-carved stairway.

Grapevine House. In front of the house, probably built in the early 1800's, are a barely visible grape arbor and a huge grapevine brought to Oxford in 1810 from the Isle of Jersey by Captain William Willis, who commanded the brig *Louisa.*

Byeberry. This is the oldest house in the area, having been built before 1695. It formerly was located in the business area and was moved to its present location on Town Creek.

Robert Morris House. At the left end of what is now an inn, located on the strand which runs along Tred Avon River, is the old home of Robert Morris, built in the 1700's. (Open)

Robert Morris House. One end of the parlor in the old house is paneled, and its fireplace is flanked by closets.

SANDY SPRING
MARYLAND

(Written by Esther B. Stabler)

The Brooke and Thomas families dominate the early history of this peaceful and prosperous Quaker town, which never knew Indian raids, military invasion, major catastrophe, or even a locomotive whistle. Now a small, substantial community some 20 miles north of Washington, D.C., it was considerably bigger in its early days when it was the only settlement for some miles around.

The first tract taken up, in 1715, was Snowden's Manor, a grant to Richard Snowden. The first settlers were James Brooke and his wife, Deborah, who came from Prince Georges County on horseback and settled on a tract called "Charley Forest." Two years later they were joined by Deborah's sister and her husband, John Thomas, who settled at nearby "Cherry Grove." Brooke eventually acquired some 20,000 acres in the area.

Both families were Quakers, and early Friends' Meetings were held in their own and neighboring homes. The Sandy Spring Meeting was established in 1753 with a house built of logs. It was succeeded in 1817 by a sturdy brick Meeting House.

The area was a virgin wilderness when the settlers came, and abounded in venison, bears, wild turkeys, and geese. The last bear in the neighborhood was not killed until 1780. Tobacco was an early crop but was later replaced by grain and dairy cattle.

From the beginning, the Quakers were a great force for good in Sandy Spring. They were greatly concerned about the condition of the Indians and worked tirelessly in the 18th century to educate them, in return for which the Indians came to trust the Quaker missionaries.

Quaker land owners also were leaders in freeing slaves, James Brooke, Jr., of "Spring Lot" being the first to do so. John Thomas of "Cherry Grove" followed suit, and Evan Thomas of "Mount Radnor" freed some 200 people, giving each family a plot of ground, a plow, a suit of clothes, and many other necessities.

Isaac Briggs opened the first school in the area in the late 1780's. Built of logs, it once stood in the corner of the present graveyard near the Meeting House.

The first boarding school was opened as early as 1800 by Samuel Thomas and his wife at "Woodlawn," and Francis Scott Key frequently rode on horseback out to Sandy Spring from Washington to visit his two daughters who boarded at the school.

Numerous descendants of the early families still live in Sandy Spring and in the nearby countryside which was once a part of the charming unincorporated town.

The Meeting House. The large, red brick Meeting House was built in 1817 and continues in regular use today. (Open)

Bloomfield. Richard Thomas built this house in about 1790 for his son. It was later occupied by Caleb Bentley, who moved to Brookeville where he gave refuge to President Madison in what is now known as the "Madison House" when the British burned the White House in 1812. The columns and end of the house are later additions.

Auburn. William Thomas, then living at "Cherry Grove," built Auburn in 1818 as a gift to his daughter. The kitchen fireplace, which has a large bake oven, measures seven feet wide, five feet high, and thirty inches deep. Over the kitchen is a weaving and carding room with exposed oak rafters.

273

The Meeting House. The center partition, which divided the men and the women, shows paneling which is the only decoration in the severely finished building.

Harewood. This house was erected in 1793 by William Stabler, who came with his wife from Virginia. The Sandy Spring Post Office was run there by Stabler's son Edward, who after 1830 held the position of Postmaster for 50 years. It is now the home of Dean Acheson, former U.S. Secretary of State.

Woodlawn. Either Richard or Samuel Thomas built this large ivy-covered, center hall, brick house in about 1774. This is where the first boarding school was located.

Woodlawn. The old kitchen fireplace with all of the early utensils now finds itself in the library.

Woodlawn. This exquisite sideboard
is seen in the dining room.

Woodlawn. The sturdy old stone barn
is known for its arched doorways.

Norwood. This also was a Richard Thomas House, built in 1751 and enlarged in 1867. Its central hall runs through to the rear, and there is a double parlor with twin fireplaces.

CHARLES TOWN

WEST VIRGINIA

Like the remainder of West Virginia, Charles Town was located in the State of Virginia from the time it was settled until 1863, when Virginia was divided into two states.

Settlers are believed to have gone to Charles Town as early as 1755. Colonel Charles Washington, George's younger brother, acquired a large acreage, including the present site of Charles Town, in 1770 and in 1786 he had 80 acres surveyed and laid out for the town, which was named for himself, as was the main thoroughfare.

Most of the early settlers were English, and members of aristocratic Tidewater Virginia families, together with the tavern keepers, blacksmiths, weavers, tailors, and coachmakers, and others required to meet their own needs. The English were followed by Germans, Scots, and Irish, who were attracted by the fertile soil.

Charles Town gradually became an educational and social community, with no early industry except two grist mills. There were numerous taverns for the entertainment of both local residents and travelers. Old Cherry, Hain's, Holl's, and Fulton were the names of some of the early establishments.

Horse shows, races, and riding tournaments were important forms of amusement in Charles Town in the early days, and even today, two race tracks are among the more important enterprises in the town.

The slave-owning aristocrats on the nearby plantations quite naturally sympathized with and supported the Southern cause when the Civil War broke out, and it is said that not a single male adult was left in town by the middle of the war. Charles Town was the scene of frequent battles. Many buildings were destroyed, and the town as a whole was battered and demoralized by the several invasions and constant troop movements.

In 1859 the Courthouse was the scene of the treason trial of the fanatical abolitionist, John Brown, and a pyramid of stones marks the site of the gallows on which he was hanged.

Mordington. Built about 1774, Mordington was the home of Colonel Charles Washington, who died there in 1797. Its massive hand-carved door with transom and sidelights is sheltered by a flat-roofed Doric portico. The two lower sections of the house were built before the higher center portion.

Crane House. This was the town house of Battaile Muse, George Washington's man of business. It was erected prior to 1800 and was later the home of Fernandino Fairfax, who inherited the title of Lord, but he renounced it.

Altona. The attractive white farmhouse was built in 1793 by Colonel Abraham Davenport and later owned by Laurence Washington, nephew of George. It was damaged by cannon fire during the Civil War but was restored.

Piedmont. Dr. John Briscoe built the conventional Georgian Colonial home in 1780. The walls of the dining room are covered by French tapestry wallpaper imported in 1802. The wallpaper design by Joseph DuFour depicts the advance of Telemarque.

Harewood. The old stone house, built in the late 1700's, was designed by George Washington for his brother Colonel Sam Washington. Dolly Paine Todd and James Madison were married there. It has an elaborate interior finish with wainscoting and moldings. Panels in the drawing room are joined upon fluted pilasters crowned with capitals.

Claymount Court. This large and impressive Georgian Colonial home is located on a rise that faces south. It was built in 1820 by Bushrod Washington, grandson of John Augustine, George Washington's third brother. Wide galleries extend the full length of the house on the first and second floors. It was destroyed by fire in 1838 and was immediately rebuilt to its original design.

Blakely. John Augustine Washington, II, brother of Bushrod, built this stately house in 1820. It faces Claymount Court to the north, across a broad expanse of open farmland. It was partly burned during the Civil War.

WINCHESTER

VIRGINIA

Located in the famed apple-growing country at the northern entrance to the Shenandoah Valley, Winchester was the locale of George Washington's first important military command. As a lieutenant colonel, he was sent to Winchester in command of frontier forces in 1755 and built Fort Loudoun to protect the town and its people against the French. However, he was no stranger to the region, having surveyed Thomas Lord Fairfax' vast holdings there, starting in 1748.

Winchester, once known as Fredericktown, had its beginnings in 1744, when James Wood laid out a courthouse square and 26 lots. The first courthouse, made of logs, was located on the present site of Glen Burnie, a large old brick home on the west side of town.

The early settlers were mostly English, but there were also many Germans who came down from the northern colonies. The General Assembly authorized the town's incorporation in 1779, after it had been officially laid out and named for Winchester, England, in 1752.

Prominent among Winchester's notable citizens was General Daniel Morgan, who fought at both Battles of Saratoga. He also was known as the hero of the Battle of Cowpens and is given credit for the defeat of British General Tarleton during the Revolution.

In the Civil War, Winchester, like neighboring Charles Town, changed hands frequently. As a result both Confederate General Stonewall Jackson and Union General Philip Sheridan had their headquarters there, the former in 1861 and the latter in 1864.

Fort Loudoun. The large structure is part of a fort built in 1756 by the then Colonel George Washington as a defense against Indians. It was named for the Earl of Loudoun, commander of the British colonial forces. (Open)

First Presbyterian Church. This simple fieldstone building was put up in 1790. Union troops used it as a stable during the Civil War.

Red Lion Tavern. The structure built of limestone was erected prior to the Revolution and for many years served as a public tavern.

Washington's Office. The little frame and stone building erected in the late 18th century served as an office for George Washington when he was doing survey work for Lord Fairfax. (Open)

Morgan House. The house was built in about 1787. General Daniel Morgan later lived there. The early part is known for its wide floor boards, paneled mantels, and massive front door lock. The old kitchen was detached.

Glen Burnie. The house was built in 1794 by Robert Wood. General James Wood, Governor of Virginia, was born there.

WATERFORD

VIRGINIA

A town which has not had any form of public transportation since stagecoach days, Waterford was settled in 1733 by Samuel Janney, a Quaker from Bucks County, Pennsylvania.

This early settler was a man of parts, for he not only founded a mill in about 1740, but also acted as a surveyor for Lord Fairfax. At about the same time, a tan yard, blacksmith shop, and several log houses were erected close to the mill.

Originally called Milltown, the community later came to be known as Waterford, thanks to the insistence of an Irish cobbler named Thomas Moore, who had emigrated from Waterford, Ireland.

After the mill was erected, a crude place of worship known as Fairfax Meeting was built of logs, the predecessor of the more substantial Meeting House which stands today on a rise outside of town. In the early building there originated what George Washington called the "Loudoun Method" of five-year crop rotation.

The community was incorporated in 1810, and a town council was formed. By 1834, Waterford was a thriving little village, consisting of about 70 houses, a tannery, a chair factory, a boot and shoe factory, and about 400 persons.

The Quakers, with their modest dwellings, found themselves wedged in, between German farmers to the north, who tilled their own lands, and English cavaliers from Tidewater Virginia, who established great estates and large mansions and started to grow tobacco with the aid of their slaves.

During the Civil War, sentiment among the people of Waterford was strongly pro-Union, but many of the Quaker residents preferred neutrality when it came to hostilities.

After the war, the village ceased expanding, and its buildings began to deteriorate until the post World War II housing shortage resulted in a welcome wave of restoration and renovation.

The Mill. Built in the early 1800's, the three-and-a-half story mill is one on which the economy of Waterford was based after it was first settled. The mill wheel lies almost submerged in the lower left hand corner of the photograph. (Open)

Old Homes. These are some of the town's 18th century houses. They were built in the vicinity of the existing mill, which appears in the background on the right.

Bond House. This handsome house, standing impressively on a corner near the mill, was erected shortly after 1800.

Loudoun Hotel. The old hotel occupied several connecting buildings put up in the late 1700's. Interior doors were built to permit movement from one portion to another.

Miriam Gover or Arch House. Recognized by the arch which leads to the rear of the property, the house was built in 1763.

288

Miriam Gover House. Under a porch is a well, which once provided the town's water supply.

Kelly House. The house located on a steep side road was erected in 1804.

289

Kelly House. The china cabinets are built-in next to the fireplace in a parlor.

Schooley House. The unusual dog-tooth brick cornice distinguishes the house built in the early 1800's.

Mays House. The brick portion of the house was erected in the late 1700's.

Mays House. Elaborate carving graces the side of the staircase.

School House. The little building was erected in 1801 by John Wickes to serve as a warehouse. Later it became a school.

Dormer House. Named for its four dormers, the house was built in the early 1800's. It became the home of J. Schooley, a miller.

FALMOUTH

VIRGINIA

A one-time riverport, Falmouth is situated on the Rappahannock River, just above the falls and across from Fredericksburg. It is quite near the spot where Captain John Smith landed in search of gold and where he fought the Indians in 1608.

The town, laid out in 1727, never grew large, having had a population of about 500 persons in the 1930's and containing no more than 1500 citizens in the early 1960's.

For a while it was a thriving port for the shipment of tobacco and flour and became sufficiently affluent in 1773 to buy a fire engine with 40 leather buckets from London.

Augustine Washington, father of George, established an iron foundry there on the bank of the river in 1732. It functioned during the Revolution making pots, pans, kettles, anchors, and bayonets for the Continental Army.

George Washington received his early schooling in Falmouth from the ages of six to eleven, while a resident of nearby Ferry Farm down the river.

Falmouth was the birthplace of James A. Seddon, Confederate Secretary of War, but even so the town was the headquarters of the Federal Army before and after the Battle of Fredericksburg.

Ferry Farm. This was George Washington's boyhood home on the bank of the Rappahannock River. It is the place where he is said to have chopped down the famous cherry tree and where he tossed a silver dollar across the river. All that is left is the old ice house and a small building where he is believed to have studied surveying. The frame house in the background is a late reproduction of the original farmhouse. (Open)

Clear View. The land was patented to Thomas Vicaris in 1703, and the house, built about 1750, was purchased in 1786 by Major Andrew Buchanan, a member of Washington's staff. Situated high on a hill, it has a majestic view of the Rappahannock River Valley and of Falmouth and Fredericksburg.

Clear View. An old portrait hangs over the mantel in the drawing room.

Clear View. The twin, back-to-back corner fireplaces are in a parlor, which at one time was divided into two separate rooms.

Carlton. Built prior to 1796, the house located on a hilltop overlooks Falmouth in the direction of Clear View. In the center hall is a handsome stairway with a balustrade that ends in a ram's head design. The dining room has built-in cupboards and interesting paneling.

295

Belmont. Now the property of Martha Washington College, Belmont was built in about 1761 by the Reverend John Dixon on a grant of 1260 acres made to Thomas Vicaris, County Clerk, for having brought 26 persons to the colony. It later was enlarged by Joseph B. Feckler and became the home of Gari Melchers, the artist. The grounds contain boxwood hedges and huge virgin oaks.

Ellerslie. Dr. Michael Wallace, who built the central portion of the house in 1748, had been indentured at the age of 15 to a doctor to learn "physical surgery" and pharmacy. Toward the end of his apprenticeship, he eloped with one of nine sisters who had 27 husbands among them. He built the house in the following year.

Gordon House. One of America's first millionaires, Basil Gordon, built this house in 1745. It is a flounder house at one end, indicating that a further addition had been contemplated.

Glebe Church. Built in colonial times, the old church was badly damaged in a storm and was bricked up just back of the facade in order to preserve the front.

Walters House. The pre-Revolutionary frame house, which has seen better days, became the home of Kate Walters Barrett, who gained prominence as an advocate of social reform.

WILLIAMSBURG

VIRGINIA

The second capital of Virginia, from 1699 to 1780, Williamsburg today is a "lively reincarnation" of a busy and important colonial town, which had fallen on bad days. While some of its old buildings are original, except for normal upkeep and modernization, the fascinating town includes 83 old buildings which have been preserved and restored and 48 important 18th century structures and many lesser places that have been faithfully reconstructed on their original foundations.

Located between the York and James Rivers, Williamsburg, thanks to its reconstruction, appears much today as it did prior to the Revolution, although 459 old buildings have been torn down.

The "Acte for the Seatinge of the Middle Plantation," as the Williamsburg area was then known, was passed in 1663, and in 1699 it was designated as the new capital of the colony, replacing Jamestown. It received the name of Williamsburg in honor of William III.

The town was incorporated in 1722 and then began to grow rapidly in size and prestige, becoming the "political and educational center of Virginia and the scene of the most 'fashionable social life' in colonial America." Balls, races, fairs, theatrical performances, and other entertainment are said to have provided an atmosphere similar to that of leading European capitals.

Williamsburg began to deteriorate when the capital was moved to Richmond to escape the British invaders in 1780. In the next few years it was occupied, first by British, and then by French and colonial forces. In 1795, the population had fallen from 2000 to 1200 persons, and the town began a slow process of decay. Little of moment occurred there until 1862 when Union forces engaged Confederates retreating from Yorktown to Richmond, and the city suffered physically at the hands of the northerners.

Then in 1926 John D. Rockefeller, Jr., lent his support to a comprehensive and unique plan for restoring the faded town to its 18th century charm and appearance, and the process of disintegration was totally reversed.

The Colonial Capitol. This is a reconstruction built on the original foundation. H-shaped, it was erected under the supervision of Henry Cary between 1701 and 1705, then was burned in 1747 and again in 1832. The General Assembly met there from 1704 to 1779, or until its removal to Richmond. (Open)

Governor's Palace. This formal dining room was used on special occasions. The heavily carved cupboard dates back to the 17th century.

Governor's Palace. On the second floor is the Upper Middle Room used by Virginia's Royal Governors and their families as a private sitting room. The bookcase, which contains appropriate editions of all books listed in Governor Boutetourt's library, is an English piece dating back to about 1740.

Brush-Everard House. John Brush, a gunsmith, armorer, and first keeper of the colony's magazine, built the town house on the Palace Green in 1717. The garden contains the oldest boxwood in Williamsburg. (Open)

Brush-Everard House. This warm room has soft green woodwork in the wainscoting and mantel. A Lowestoft tea set is on the table and 18th century figurines stand on the mantel.

Brush-Everard House. The library in this modest home contains a unique collection of books assembled from a list compiled by Thomas Jefferson in 1771 for the guidance of a well-to-do gentleman.

Sir John and Peyton Randolph House. The long frame dwelling, built as two houses in about 1715, was bought in 1724 by Sir John Randolph, an economist, who served as Virginia's representative in London. His son, Peyton, who inherited the house, was chairman of Virginia's first three conventions and first President of the First Continental Congress. Generals Rochambeau and Lafayette used the house as their headquarters before the siege of Yorktown.

Carter-Saunders House. The first owner of this stately house, built prior to 1746, was Charles Carter, son of Robert "King" Carter. George Washington, Governor Boutetourt, and Governor Eden of North Carolina were among the many distinguished guests entertained there. It has been faithfully restored.

George Wythe House. Colonel Richard Taliaferro, an architect, is believed to have built the house in 1755 and left it to George Wythe, his son-in-law. Wythe was the first professor of law in America and a teacher of Thomas Jefferson, John Marshall, James Monroe, and Henry Clay. It was Washington's headquarters before the siege of Yorktown. Jefferson lived there for a month in 1776, and Rochambeau occupied it after the siege. (Open)

Wythe House. The dining room is dominated by the portrait of St. George Tucker, who succeeded Wythe as professor of law. The portrait is attributed to William Hubbard. The three-sectioned cherry dining table and the mahogany chairs are American pieces of the late 18th century.

Wythe House. Here in the northeast bedroom, one of four, are rare bed hangings of red and white English copperplate, stamped "R. Jones, 1761."

Governor's Palace. This is a faithful reproduction of the early residence of the Royal Governors, started in 1705 under Henry Cary and completed in 1720. It is surrounded by ten formal gardens. Its interior is noted for exquisite woodwork, especially in the wide entrance hall and most of the passages. The walls of the library are covered with antique Spanish tooled leather. The building was burned in 1781 while being used as a hospital for Continental soldiers wounded at Yorktown. It was badly damaged by Union troops in 1863. (Open)

The Colonial Capitol. The Governor and his Council performed their judicial functions as the General Court. Here they served as a Court of Appeals and, in certain cases, as a Court of General Jurisdiction. The General Court chamber occupies the lower floor of the west wing. It was in this chamber that Black-beard's pirates and other notorious criminals received their sentences.

The Colonial Capitol. In this room, the House of Burgesses, the oldest legislative assembly in America, held its meetings from 1704 to 1780. At the far end of the room is the Speaker's chair, in which the Speaker of the House attempted to stop Patrick Henry during his famous "Caesar-Brutus" speech.

Raleigh Tavern. The L-shaped building with its many dormers was built before 1742 and has been completely reconstructed, after being burned in 1859. The Apollo Room was a frequent rendezvous of Revolutionary patriots, including Thomas Jefferson and Patrick Henry. It was once owned by John Blair, and its first known inn-keeper was Henry Wetherburn. The Phi Beta Kappa honorary society was formed in the Apollo Room.

Raleigh Tavern. In this kitchen meals were prepared for many colonial greats. Game is seen hanging from a meat ring. It is furnished with antique mixing and cooking utensils.

JAMESTOWN

VIRGINIA

Often referred to as the first "permanent" English settlement in the New World, Jamestown endured only about 90 years until it was virtually deserted, after its statehouse had burned and Williamsburg had succeeded it as the colonial capital in 1699.

Following unsuccessful attempts to settle in the Virginia area by Sir Humphrey Gilbert and Sir Walter Raleigh, three small ships—the *Susan Constant, Godspeed,* and *Discovery*—brought colonists to Jamestown on the James River in 1607. An early leader was Captain John Smith, who is credited with holding the colony together during its first difficult two-and-a-half years, before he returned to England following a serious injury.

During the early months, nine-tenths of the colonists died, the victims of sickness and hunger. The survivors were so discouraged that they planned to depart and actually had made a start, but turned back when they learned of the timely arrival of the newly appointed governor, Lord De La Ware, who brought men and supplies.

From then on, things looked up and a small town was established. Plantations were developed and, in about 1610–11, the economy was strengthened when the culture of tobacco proved successful. The leader in that development was John Rolfe, who later married Pocahontas, daughter of the Indian Chief Powhatan, thus helping to bring about a period of peace with the Indians.

Although settlements spread out along the James River, Jamestown became the early political, social, and economic center of the colony.

However, the town was burned in 1676 during a revolt against the constituted authority. It was soon rebuilt, but then the Statehouse was burned in 1698. As a result, the capital was moved to Williamsburg and the town gradually disintegrated. Now it is part of a National Historical Site, with none of its early buildings remaining; only ruins and recent monuments attest to its historic significance.

The Tercentenary Monument. The 103-foot granite shaft was erected in 1907 to commemorate the 300th anniversary of the settlement.

Pocahontas Statue. This bronze statue honors the Indian girl who warned the settlers against attacks by her people and who is credited with saving the life of Captain John Smith with whom she fell in love without his knowledge, before she married John Rolfe.

Jamestown Church Tower. The only standing relic of the first English settlement is a bulky, ivy-draped brick ruin of an old church, whose construction was started in 1639. A memorial church adjoining the ruin was built early in the 20th century on the foundations of the early church.

John Smith Statue. This bronze figure, overlooking the broad James River, honors Captain John Smith, the forceful leader who held the settlers together in their early days of hardship.

Moore House. This is a restored house built by Augustine Moore in 1725, in which the terms of the British surrender were arranged after the fighting in Yorktown in 1781 was terminated. The signatories were, for the British: Cornwallis, and Thomas Symonds; for the Continental Army, "G. Washington, Le Comte de Rochambeau, and Le Comte de Barras, for himself and for Le Comte de Grasse." The house has a slight overhang with a decorative cornice. (Open)

YORKTOWN
VIRGINIA

Three wars brought excitement to Yorktown, although the village did not see heavy fighting in any of them. It is located atop a high bluff on the south bank of the York River, in what is now Colonial National Historic Park. A town at the site of Yorktown was authorized as a port in 1680 by the General Assembly.

In 1781, when Lord Cornwallis found himself faced with the combined armies of Washington, Rochambeau, and Lafayette, he decided to fortify Yorktown as a base for contact with the British fleet and brought his army there by water.

However, the French fleet under the Comte de Grasse, sailing up from the West Indies, met the British fleet outside the Virginia Capes and forced it to retire. The American and French forces then surrounded Yorktown, making surrender inevitable. After a bombardment lasting a week, Cornwallis attempted to take his troops across the York River, but was thwarted by a storm. The surrender came the following day, after relatively few casualties.

In 1814, Yorktown, guarded by militia, was threatened by a British fleet but nothing serious occurred. In 1862, the Confederates led by General John B. Magruder fortified the town, but they were forced out by Federal troops under the command of General George B. McClellan.

Congress authorized the construction of a marble monument on the battlefield of 1781, but a century elapsed before another Congress appropriated the money for a 95 foot shaft bearing a figure of Liberty with arms outstretched.

Moore House. A splendid old secretary and table are among the antiques to be enjoyed in the parlor.

Moore House. More graceful old furniture is seen in the dining room.

Scheild (Sessions) House. Thomas Sessions built this house, the oldest in Yorktown, prior to 1699. It contains many fine pieces of Chippendale furniture, old silver and copper lustre. The front door is eight feet high and contains eight beaded panels. The stairway is in the back and there are marble mantels.

Nelson House. The brick wall on the east end of the house shows two cannon balls, which presumably are marks of the bombardment directed by the owner against the British. Finished in the mid-1730's, it was the home of Governor Thomas Nelson and later was the headquarters of Cornwallis. The drawing room located off the transverse hall has engaged columns to frame the opening. The house has high ceilings, tall windows, and low doors.

Nelson House. A beautiful formal garden surrounds the house on two sides, with crepe myrtle and azaleas blooming in profusion.

Smith House. The house is named for its builder, Edward Smith, who had it under construction at the time of his death in 1750.

Thomas Pate (Cole Digges) House.
The house was built in the early 1700's
by John Martin and later sold to Cole
Digges. It has high, pine-paneled ceilings.

Grace Church. The walls of the little
church are made of marl, which has been
hardened by the fires that have ravaged
the building. It was started about 1697.
The communion set was presented by
Nathaniel Bacon, Sr., in 1649 to Hampton Parish in York County and was used
there until this church was built. The
interior was burned during the Revolution, when the British used it as a magazine, and again in 1814. It also was used
for military purposes in 1860 and had a
signal tower on its roof. (Open)

Grace Church. The Sign of the Cross is repeated in the long paneled wall back of the altar.

Bonner House. From the densely shaded front porch of the house, there is a sweeping view of Bath Creek and Back Creek, looking toward Blackbeard's headquarters. It was built about 1750. A fort in the back yard, from which the photograph was made, defended the town during the war with the Tuscarora Indians. (Open)

BATH TOWN

NORTH CAROLINA

For its size—Bath Town has fewer than 400 inhabitants—it has an impressive history. Across Back Creek is Plum Point, the place where Blackbeard, the pirate, used to have his home and his headquarters, and across Bath Creek were the homes of former Governors Eden and Daniel, who made Bath Town their seat of government. Former Governor Cary lived on the edge of town. Another Royal Governor, Matthew Rowan, had been a merchant in Bath Town.

English settlers went to the Bath Town area in about 1695, eleven years after the first proprietory grant was made in the vicinity. David Perkins, whose farm included the present site of the town, was among the first settlers.

In 1704, he sold 60 acres of his farm to John Lawson, Joel Martin, and Simon Alderson, and in the following year the town was incorporated with those three men as its founders and first Commissioners.

Bath Town was the site of the Cary rebellion and a place of refuge for settlers who survived the attack by the Tuscarora Indians on New Bern. In 1729, the General Assembly authorized 145 acres east of the town gate as a common grazing plot for livestock owned by local citizens.

The General Assembly met there in 1744 and in 1752, and in 1746 the Lower House of the Assembly passed an Act designating Bath as the first permanent capital of North Carolina. Neither the Council nor the Governor approved the Act, so it did not become law.

Bonner House. A graceful, hand-carved mantel stands back of the sturdy dining room table.

Bonner House. The heavy, hand-hewn rafters and original roof boards are exposed in the attic.

Glebe House. This is said to be the only house built for a preacher by the Church in the entire colony. The first minister to ever live in it was Parson Alexander Stewart, who occupied it during the year it was built, 1750. It is located in front of St. Thomas Church.

St. Thomas Church. Situated back from the main street, the Parish Church of the Bishop of East Carolina was built in 1734. It possesses a bell given by Queen Anne, three-branch candlesticks said to have been given by King George II in about 1740, and a large silver chalice given by the Bishop of London to the Reverend John Gargia, first resident rector of the Parish. (Open)

Buzzard Hotel. The elderly, unpainted frame structure was erected in about 1740 and named for its builder and operator.

Palmer-Marsh House. Captain Michael Coutanch, a native of the Isle of Jersey, built this, the largest existing house in Bath Town, in 1744. In 1764, Captain Robert Palmer, the surveyor general of the colony and a member of the Governor's Council, bought the house. Then in 1782, it was purchased by Jonathan and Daniel G. Marsh and remained in the family for over 100 years. The General Assembly met there in 1744 and 1752, and it is claimed locally that it once housed the first public library in the United States. (Open)

Palmer-Marsh House. A handsome desk and old chairs are placed in the library.

Palmer-Marsh House. The early drop-leaf table rests below a wide chair rail in the dining room.

Palmer-Marsh House. Near the four-poster is an old-fashioned rack used to dry clothes and hold towels.

Old Foundations. Twelve of the 60 foundations uncovered by archeologists have been excavated, and once devasted Brunswick has become an historic site of North Carolina. This old building looked out over the Cape Fear River.

BRUNSWICK
NORTH CAROLINA

Only the partial walls of an old church and foundations of buildings excavated by archeologists remain of the once major shipping port named after the Prince of Brunswick. Prior to its burning by the British in 1776, the town on the Cape Fear River had perhaps 100 homes and other buildings.

It was founded in 1725 by Colonel Maurice Moore, who had visited the site at the head of a relief force after the Tuscarora massacres in 1711. It was a county seat in the 1730's, and the North Carolina Assembly met there frequently during the period when Royal Governors Arthur Dobbs and William Tryon resided there. However, Governor Gabriel Johnson had moved the courts, Council, and port offices to Wilmington in 1735.

Spanish sailors siezed the town and occupied it for three days in 1748. They had partly destroyed it before it was recaptured by citizens led by William Day.

In 1765, a group of townspeople led by Cornelius Harnett surrounded the home of Governor Tryon in protest against the Stamp Act and placed the Governor under house arrest. The use of arms on this occasion was one of the first instances of armed resistance to British authority in the colonies.

After the Revolutionary War began, the residents feared that British ships and the war would destroy the town, so they moved away. Their fears were borne out in 1776 when Brunswick was burned by British sailors. After the war, only a few families chose to move back. Because the buildings had been destroyed and because the harbor had proved to be unsafe in stormy weather and too exposed to pirate attack, many former citizens elected not to return to Brunswick. By 1830, the town was totally in ruins.

Old Foundations. Stones gathered in the vicinity served to construct the foundations of the early houses.

Old Foundations. Most of the houses in the old town appear to have been comparatively small, but undoubtedly the residences of the governors were larger.

St. Philip's Church. This is Brunswick's most impressive ruin. Built in 1765, it was His Majesty's Chapel in the colony, and in it Royal Governors Dobbs and Tryon had their pews, raised above the others.

St. Philip's Church. The brick walls of the church were 33 inches thick, and the chancel windows were 15 feet high and seven feet wide.

HILLSBOROUGH

NORTH CAROLINA

The hanging in 1771 of six Regulators, a group of farmers who thought that the back country should have better representation at the state capital and that taxes and other fees should be fairly imposed and honestly collected, is a high spot in Hillsborough's early history.

Otherwise, the little town escaped armed violence, although Lord Cornwallis encamped there for five days with his British troops in 1781.

Prominent citizens were William Hooper, a signer of the Declaration of Independence, State Chief Justice Thomas Ruffin, and Associate U.S. Supreme Court Justice Alfred Moore.

When Hillsborough was platted on 400 acres in 1754 by William Churton, it was known as Orange and later was called Corbinton and Childsburg. It finally was renamed to honor the Earl of Hillsborough, an Irish peer. Located in a valley on the Eno River, it had been the home of the Haw, Eno, and Occoneechee Indians.

It was the temporary capital of North Carolina during the Revolution and the meeting place of the Third Provincial Congress, three General Assemblies, and the Constitutional Convention of 1788, which, while failing to ratify the new Federal Constitution, nevertheless did recommend that a Bill of Rights be appended to it.

Almost the entire population is descended from the Scotch-Irish, Welsh, English, and Germans who settled there at an early date.

Ayr Mount. William Kirkland, a merchant and planter from Scotland, built the tall brick house, in which members of the family resided for more than 160 years after it was erected in about 1780–1800. It has lateral halls 40 feet long, with winding staircases, and five rooms 25 feet square with ceilings 13½ feet high, plus excellent paneling.

Nash-Hooper House. The rear part of the house probably was started in 1768 by Isaac Edwards, the front block in 1772 by Francis Nash. It later was the home of William Hooper, the signer, and Governor William A. Graham.

Nash-Hooper House. The kitchen, though modernized, has a good deal of old pine in the mantel and elsewhere.

Murphy House. The rambling house, built on five levels, is believed to have been built prior to 1800, by Barnaby Cabe. It has reeded mantels and an arched fireplace in the cellar.

Courtney House. The modest, square dwelling is thought to have been erected prior to 1768 by Benjamin Merritt and was acquired by William Cornwallis, a Quaker, in 1772. Original paneling and moldings remain.

Regulators' Marker. A marker and a slab, enclosed by an iron fence, mark the spot where the six Regulators were hanged after three years of agitation. Their graves are nearby. The Regulator movement is regarded locally as an important preliminary step in the American Revolution.

Courthouse Clock. Although the present courthouse was not built until 1844, the clock in the cupola was made in Birmingham, England, and is thought to have been a Royal gift to the town in about 1769. Earlier it is said to have hung in a church tower.

Forest House. The pre-Revolutionary house formerly was the town Post Office. It belonged to Roswell Huntington, a silversmith. Although relatively small, it has massive twin chimneys on each end and pine wainscoting and mantels.

Chatwood. The early part of the house was a tavern, probably built in about 1790 by Robert Faucett. The old tap-room is now the kitchen.

Chatwood. Random width pine boards line the parlor on all four sides and on the ceiling and floor.

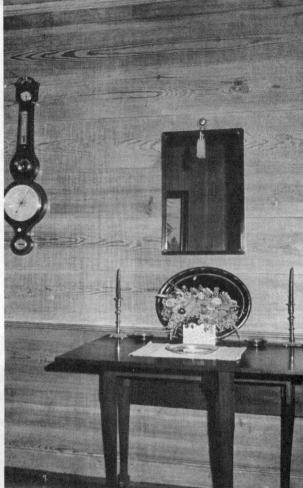

Chatwood. The parlor has unusual horizontal paneling back of the fine corner cupboard. Vertical wall boards are seen in other rooms.

Moorefields. The house with its beautiful Chinese Chippendale staircase was erected in 1785 by Justice Moore, as his summer home. The two-story central block has flanking wings. The house has its original hardware and a fine overmantel.

OLD SALEM

NORTH CAROLINA

Now a part of the thriving city of Winston-Salem, the original backwoods town with its distinct old world atmosphere and charm was settled in 1766 by Moravians who were followers of the pre-Reformation leader, John Hus, who was burned at the stake in 1415. It was a trading point for frontiersmen and a stopping place for pioneers on the westward drive.

Principally, however, Salem was a religious town, with the congregation owning the land and supervising all crafts and industries through elected officials.

Salem settlers, reared in the artisan culture of their native Germany, were skilled craftsmen, turning out a variety of wares, such as pottery, leather goods, guns, silverware, and clocks. Culturally, they were more advanced than most early groups and had excellent schools.

The little town was a planned community, mid-European in style, with buildings constructed close to the walks and clustered around a central square.

More than half of the original buildings are still standing and in use. A nonprofit educational organization known as Old Salem, Inc., laudably has undertaken to restore the buildings that remain and return them authentically to their early appearance and purposes. To date, eight buildings have been restored and already most are open to the public, enabling the visitor to visualize early Moravian life in the fascinating town.

During the Revolution, Old Salem was a vital supply base for Continental troops, and Traugott Bagge, a Salem merchant, acted as purchasing agent for the army.

Home Moravian Church. Built in 1800, the stately edifice still serves the largest Moravian congregation in America. Among its interesting architectural details are the octagonal cupola, the clock, the hooded doorway, and the graceful iron railings which never have rusted. (Open)

The Boys' School. The old school-house, now a part of Wachovia Museum, was erected in 1794. It is considered a fine example of Moravian ornamental brick construction and has its original tile roof. The museum contains a large collection of local artifacts and antiquities. (Open)

The Tobacco Shop. This was the home, workshop, and store of Matthew Miksch, tobacconist. It was built in 1771 and was the first privately-owned house in Old Salem, originally containing two rooms—a kitchen and general living room on either side of a central chimney. It is believed to be the oldest tobacco shop standing in America today. (Open)

The Tobacco Shop. This sturdy old furniture is placed in the living room.

The Tobacco Shop. On these shelves are examples of the tobacco products that Miksch manufactured in his shop. The little jars above contain snuff. On the left end of the shelf below are coils of chewing tobacco, and containers of pipe tobacco are on the third shelf.

The Tobacco Shop. A flax wheel and clock-reel for winding yarn stand close to the handsome wardrobe in the small bedroom.

The Tobacco Shop. Aside from the collection of old silver and early utensils, the backless chairs around the dining table stand out in the kitchen.

The Brothers' House. The half-timbered portion of the house, a section of which is shown in the photograph, was constructed in 1769. This is where the unmarried men of the community lived from the age of 14, when they were apprenticed to master craftsmen to learn a trade. Two floors of splendid exhibits, including a well-equipped gunsmith's shop and a shoemaker's shop, have been readied for the public. (Open)

John Vogler House. An interesting canopy, identifying the owner as a clockmaker, is seen on the house built in 1819. The interior furnishings include many pieces which belonged to the first owner, who also was a silversmith. (Open)

337

John Vogler House. Two Moravian ear-wing chairs are drawn up by the fireplace, above which are portraits of John Vogler and his wife, Christina. Other early furnishings include a music stand, homemade violin, and bellows.

Christoph Vogler House. The original owner of the house, built in 1797 and the oldest brick building in Salem, was the village gunsmith. It was constructed by Johann Gottlieb Kraus, master builder.

Salem Tavern. In 1791, George Washington was a two-day visitor in the tavern erected in 1784. It was owned by the Congregation and operated by a church-appointed keeper, who sometimes tended bar. It could house as many as 40 guests. (Open)

Salem Tavern. Up to 40 persons could be served at each meal prepared in this large kitchen with its twin fireplaces. An interesting assortment of kitchen utensils can be seen in the oak-beamed kitchen.

Salem Tavern. In a corner of the kitchen, near the stairs, fowl hang to ripen, and herbs are drying above the candle-dipping wheel.

Salem Tavern. Quaint wooden chairs stand on each side of the corner cupboard, filled with early china.

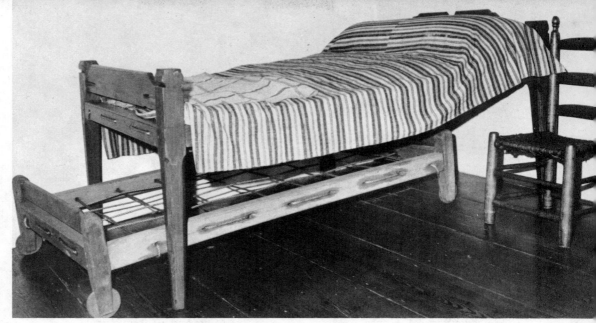

Salem Tavern. There is nothing luxurious about the narrow bed and trundle bed, with their rope springs, seen in a second-floor bedroom.

Lick-Boner House. Martin Lick, an early carpenter, built this house which represents the simple style of dwelling in the old village. It dates from 1787. John Henry Boner, a poet, was born here.

341

APPENDIX

Locations of Places
Named in Text

WISCASSET

Lee-Payson-Smith House	High Street, across from Library
Nickels-Sortwell House	Main and Federal Streets
Thomas W. Smith House	Washington and Federal Streets
Lilac Cottage	Facing common
Marsten House	Main and Middle Streets
Merean House	Main and Pleasant Streets
Taylor House	Main and Hodge Streets

YORK VILLAGE

Coventry Hall	Just east of town on road to York Beach
Woodbridge	Across from Coventry Hall
The Pillory	In front of Old Jail
Hugh Holmes House	In town
Old School	Near old tavern
Steven Lovejoy House	On road to Kittery
John Hancock Wharf	On waterfront
Elizabeth Perkins House	On road to Kittery, just before long bridge

DURHAM

Demerritt Homestead	Near Madbury
Valentine Smith House	Main Street, east of Post Office
Ebeneezer Smith House	Next to Valentine Smith House
Judge Frost House	On hill above near bank of river
Yatten	Between Frost House and river
General Sullivan House	Near far bank of river

EXETER

Governor Weare House	On Exeter Road in Hampton Falls
Garrison House	Water and Clifford Streets
Congregational Church	Front Street near Water Street
Benjamin Clark Gilman House	39 Front Street
First Academy Building	Tan Lane
Ladd-Gilman House	Water Street and Governor Lane
Lyford Farmhouse	Out Water Street extended

WOODSTOCK

Dana House	Elm Street
Swan House	37 Elm Street
Kidder House	Elm Street
Hutchinson House	One The Green
Richards House	9 The Green
William Dimon House	21 The Green
Parker House	26 The Green

MANCHESTER

Old Tavern	On US 7 in Manchester Center
Grist Mill	On US 7 in Manchester Center
1811 Tavern	On US 7 in town
Equinox House	On US 7 in town
Hoyt House	On US 7 in town
Hard Homestead	Southeast of town on valley road
Hard House	On US 7 south of town

BENNINGTON

Governor Galusha House	On US 7 north of Shaftsbury
Monroe-Hawkins House	On US 7 south of Galusha House
Frost House	.9 mi. south of Monroe-Hawkins House
Battle Monument	At top of Monument Road
Robinson House	South of Monument on Monument Road
First Congregational Church	On Monument Road
Dewey House	South of Church
Walloomsac Inn	Across from Church
Tichenor Mansion	Back of Inn on S 9

OLD NEWBURY

Short House	On S 1A in Newbury
Coffin House	On S 1A north of Short House
Cushing House	98 High Street
Pettingell-Fowler House	180 High Street
Mosely House	182 High Street
Jackson-Dexter House	201 High Street
Courthouse	On the Mall
Old Jail	Aubin Street, west of High Street

ANDOVER

Isaac Abbot Tavern	70 Elm Street
Samuel Abbot House	47 Central Street
John Lovejoy Abbot House	57 Central Street
Solomon Higgins-Abbot House	59 Central Street
Bulfinch Hall	On the campus
Pearson Hall	On the campus
Moses Stuart House	215 Main Street
Blanchard House	97 Main Street
Poor-Perry House	68 Phillips Street
Abbot Homestead	Andover Street and Argilla Road

MARBLEHEAD

Pitcher House	42 Orne Street
Orne House	18 Orne Street
Barnard House	7 Franklin Street
Devereux House	16 Franklin Street
Glover House	11 Glover Street
Old Town House	Market Square
St. Michael's Church	Summer Street near Square
Lafayette House	Union Street
Colonel Jeremiah Lee House	161 Washington Street
Hooper-Parker House	181 Washington Street
Colonel William R. Lee House	185 Washington Street
Powder House	37 Green Street

DANVERS

Fowler House	165 High Street
Rebecca Nurse House	149 Pine Street
Judge Holten House	171 Holten Street

Joseph Holten House	27 Centre Street
Haines House	35 Centre Street
Wadsworth House	73 Centre Street
Upton Tavern	95 Centre Street
Page House	11 Page Street
The Lindens	In Washington, D.C.

LEXINGTON

Milliken House	1377 Massachusetts Avenue
Buckman Tavern	1 Bedford Street
Hancock-Clarke House	35 Hancock Street
Fiske House	63 Hancock Street
Jonathan Harrington Jr. House	1 Harrington Road
L. Harrington House	5 Harrington Road
Monroe House	1906 Massachusetts Avenue
Minute Man Statue	Near the Battle Green

CONCORD

The Wayside	Lexington Road
Orchard House	Lexington Road and Cambridge Turnpike
Antiquarian House	Lexington Road
Brown House	27 Lexington Road
Wright Tavern	2 Lexington Road
Colonial Inn	11 Massachusetts Square
The Old Manse	Monument Street next to Battleground
Minute Man Statue	On Battleground

DEDHAM

Fairbanks House	East Street and Eastern Avenue
Powder House	Across from 163 Ames Street
Haven House	669 High Street
First Church	On Church Green on High Street
Congregational Church	Across from First Church
Dexter House	699 High Street

PLYMOUTH

Antiquarian House	126 Water Street
Plackett House	Near Plymouth Hall
Winslow House	Main and North Streets
Spooner House	27 North Street

Leonard House	South side of Leyden Street
Old Town House	South side of Town Square
Sparrow House	Summer and Spring Streets
Bonum House	Summer Street across from Sparrow House
Harlow House	119 Sandwich Street
Kendall-Holmes House	8 Winter Street

OLD DEERFIELD

Obtain map locally

NORTHAMPTON

Smith Homestead	Main Street in Hatfield Center
Parsons House	58 Bridge Street
Damon House	46 Bridge Street
Wiggins Tavern	Court Street in center of town
Sessions House	Elm Street on Campus

HADLEY

Porter-Phelps-Huntington House	2.2 mi. north on S 63
Eleazar Porter House	West Street
Farm Museum	Near Congregational Church
Congregational Church	Middle Street
Allen Tavern	Middle Street

EAST GREENWICH

White Swan Tavern	4365 Post Road, north of town
Greene House	86 Main Street
Kent County Courthouse	Main and Court Streets
Captain John Congdon House	Division Street near Pierce Street
Eldredge House	Division and Pierce Streets
Windmill House	144 Division Street
Varnum House	57 Pierce Street

STONINGTON

Denison House	Pequot Trail
Palmer House	14 Elm Street
Amos Palmer House	24 Main Street
Edmund Fanning House	44 Main Street
Gilbert Fanning House	38 Main Street
Pendleton House	1 Main Street

Ash House   5 Main Street
Cannon Square   On the waterfront

WINDSOR

Ellsworth Homestead   778 Palisado
Stoughton House   546 Palisado
Chaffee House   108 Palisado
Fyler House   96 Palisado

WETHERSFIELD

Buttolph-Williams House   249 Broad Street
Congregational Church   Main and Marsh Streets
Deane House   203 Main Street
Webb House   211 Main Street
The Academy   150 Main Street
Ashbul Wright House   133 Main Street
Latimer House   493 Main Street

FARMINGTON

Stanley-Whitman House   High Street south of Farmington Avenue
Thompson House   High Street north of Stanley-Whitman House
Judd House   High Street north of Thompson House
Whitman Tavern   High Street across from Judd House
Elm Tree Inn   Farmington Avenue near Main Street
Congregational Church   Main Street south of Farmington Avenue
101 Main Street   101 Main Street

LITCHFIELD

Allen House   West side of North Street
Sheldon's Tavern   West side of North Street
Tallmadge House   West side of North Street
Deming House   East side of North Street
Corner House   East side of North Street at the Green
Apothecary Shop   On the Green
Samuel Seymour House   West side of South Street
Tapping Reeve House   West side of South Street
Law School   In garden of Reeve House
Oliver Wolcott Sr. House   East side of South Street
Oliver Wolcott Jr. House   West side of South Street

WOODBURY

St. Paul's Church	On US 6
The Rectory	West of Church
Bacon House	Hollow Road
Curtis Store	Next to Bacon House
The Glebe	Hollow Road
Curtis House	US 6 just west of town

MORRISTOWN

Ford House	230 Morris Avenue
Dr. Jabez Campbell House	5 Olyphant Street
Mills House	27 Mills Street
Wick House	Jockey Hollow
Army Hospital	Jockey Hollow
Vail House	.9 mi. north of Morris Plains on US 202

PRINCETON

Berrien House	2.7 mi. north on US 27, left 2 mi.
Quaker Meeting House	1 mi. out Mercer Street
Thomas Clark Farmhouse	Off Mercer Street nearer town
Beatty House	19 Van Deventer Street
Nassau Hall	On Campus
Revolutionary Cannon	Back of Nassau Hall
Battle Monument	Intersection of Stockton, Mercer, and Nassau Streets
Morven	Stockton Street and Library Place
Alexander Hall	Elm Drive near Nassau Street
Thomas Olden House	On US 206, .9 mi. south

BORDENTOWN

Joseph Hopkinson House	Park and Third Streets
Hoagland's Tavern	Park and Farnsworth Streets
Borden House	Park and Farnsworth Streets
Francis Hopkinson House	Park and Farnsworth Streets
Patience Wright House	Park and Farnsworth Streets
Thomas Paine House	Church and Farnsworth Streets
Hilton House	100 Walnut Street

SALEM

Joseph Darkin House	Southwest of town
Isaac Smart House	Southwest of town
Holmeland	Southwest of town
Guilford House	1 Johnson Street
Jones Law Office	Across from Grant House, back of County Building
Grant House	79 Market Street
Salem Oak	West Broadway at Oak Street
Hancock House	At Hancock's Bridge
Alloways Creek Meeting House	Near Hancock House

WASHINGTON CROSSING

Point of embarkation	In State Park
Grist Mill	In State Park
Thompson-Neely House	In State Park
Dr. Chapman House	Get map in Thompson-Neely House
Merrick House	Get map in Thompson-Neely House
Hayhurst	Get map in Thompson-Neely House

NEW CASTLE

Immanuel Church	Harmony and Market Streets
The Academy	Third and Harmony Streets
Read House	The Strand near Harmony Street
Van Leuvenigh House	2 The Strand
Bedford House	6 The Strand
Courthouse	Delaware Street at the Green
Old Dutch House	32 E. Third Street
Kensey Johns Sr. House	300 Delaware Street
Senator Nicholas Van Dyke House	400 Delaware Street

DOVER

Aspendale	Just west of Kenton on S 300
The Paton House	Northwest corner of the Green
Old State House	At the head of the Green
Sykes House	Southeast corner of the Green
Bradford-Loockerman House	419 S. State Street
The Old Academy	529 S. State Street
Dickinson Mansion	East of US 113 on S 68, left .25 mi.

LEWES

Cannon Ball House	Front Street near Market Street
Maull House	Pilot Town Road before Rodney Avenue
Fisher House	Pilot Town Road past Rodney Avenue
Methodist Meeting House	Third and Mulberry Streets
Hall House	Kings Highway and Third Street
Hitchens House	Kings Highway between Madison and Monroe Streets

ELKTON

Graymount	North of town on top of hill
The Hermitage	259 E. Main Street
Mitchell House	E. Main Street, west of Church Street
Partridge Hall	Bow Street
Hollingsworth Tavern	W. Main Street, west of bridge
Gilpin Manor	1.1 mi. west on S 279

CHESTER TOWN

Rock of Ages	532 High Street
White Swan Tavern	231 High Street
Wickes House	High and Front Streets
Widehall	High and Front Streets
Custom House	101 Front Street

EASTON

Hughlett Henry House	26 South Street
Old Frame Hotel	Washington and Goldsborough Streets
Brick Hotel	Washington and Federal Streets
Talbot County Courthouse	Washington and Dover Streets
Historical Society House	26 S. Washington Street
Third Haven Meeting House	S. Washington Street
Ratcliffe Manor	1.1 mi. west on S 33, south .7 mi.
Old Bloomfield	3.3 mi. west on S 33, south 1.1 mi.

ST. MICHAELS

The Inn	Talbot and Mulberry Streets
St. Mary's Square	E. end of Talbot Street
Amelia Welby House	Mulberry Street, across from Cannon Ball House
Cannon Ball House	Mulberry Street, west of Square

Log Houses	Mill Street, near Cedar Alley
Crooked Intention	Just south of railroad
Mt. Misery	South of Crooked Intention
San Domingo	East of Mt. Misery

OXFORD

Combesbury	.3 mi. south on Evergreen Road
Plimhimmon	.9 mi. west of Evergreen Road
Tilghman Monument	East edge of town, in front of Plimhimmon
Barnaby House	Morris Street
Grapevine House	Morris Street near center of town
Byeberry	On Town Creek
Robert Morris House	Morris Street and The Strand

SANDY SPRING

Bloomfield	East edge of town, north of S 108
Auburn	Adjacent to Meeting House
The Meeting House	South of the Bank
Harewood	South of Meeting House
Woodlawn	On Dr. Bird Road
Norwood	On Dr. Bird Road, west of Woodlawn

CHARLES TOWN

Crane House	E. Washington and S. Samuel Streets
Mordington	South end of Mordington Lane
Altona	1.2 mi. west on S 51
Piedmont	Between Altona and Harewood
Harewood	3.3 mi. west on S 51
Blakely	1.8 mi. south on US 340, then right 1.6 mi.
Claymount Court	North of Blakely

WINCHESTER

Fort Loudoun	Loudoun and Clark Streets
First Presbyterian Church	304 E. Picadilly Street
Red Lion Tavern	Cork and Loudoun Streets
Washington's Office	Cork and Braddock Streets
Morgan House	226 W. Amherst Street
Glen Burnie	W. Amherst Street near City Limits

WATERFORD

Inquire locally

FALMOUTH

Ferry Farm	1.0 mi. east on S 3
Clear View	On a hill on east edge of town
Carlton	West on US 17, turn right to top of hill
Belmont	West on US 17, turn south opposite Carlton
Ellerslie	2.0 mi. west on R 652, turn left
Gordon House	Downtown on river
Glebe Church	On rise east of US 1
Walters House	2 blocks north of Church

WILLIAMSBURG

Get tourist map locally

JAMESTOWN

In National Park

YORKTOWN

Moore House	East of town in National Park
Scheild House	Main Street east of Nelson House
Nelson House	Main Street west of Custom House
Smith House	South of Nelson House
Pate House	Main Street across from Nelson House
Grace Church	Between Main Street and river

BATH TOWN

Bonner House	South end of Main Street
Glebe House	Main Street north of Bonner House
St. Thomas Church	Back of the Glebe
Buzzard Hotel	Main Street north of the Glebe
Palmer-Marsh House	Main Street north of the hotel

BRUNSWICK

Inquire locally

HILLSBOROUGH

Ayr Mount	9 mi. east on St. Mary's Road, turn right .3 mi.
Nash-Hooper House	118 W. Tryon Street
Murphy House	157 E. King Street

Courtney House	141 E. King Street
Regulators' Marker	East end of King Street, back of Church
Courthouse Clock	King and Churton Streets
Chatwood	.8 mi. west on US 70, turn right 2 mi. on Faucett Road
Moorefields	2.1 mi. west of Courthouse on Dimmocks Mill Road

OLD SALEM

Home Moravian Church	Center of town, east of Main Street
Boys' School	S. Main and Academy Streets
Tobacco Shop	S. Main Street, north of Academy Street
Brothers' House	600 S. Main Street
John Vogler House	700 S. Main Street
Christoph Vogler House	708 S. Main Street
Salem Tavern	800 S. Main Street
Lick-Boner House	512 S. Salt Street